This book is dedicated to my mother Mary Ellen Melesko, and to the memory of my father, Thomas Hawkins Kraft, whose personal sacrifices allowed me to begin my musical journey.

Special thanks to:

My wife Heidi Kraft for her unwavering support

La Bella Strings for their continued support (www.labella.com)

Sophie Pope for proofing the material (www.sophiepope.com)

Sabine Kunz for helping to bring my cover concept to life

Justin Stewart for realizing my logo (www.justin3000.com)

Thank you:

Family, friends, fans and former teachers near and far, past and present, for your friendship, inspiration, support and guidance

© 2015 kraftytoonz
All rights reserved

Unauthorized copying, arranging, adapting, recording or public performance is an infringement of copyright. Infringers are liable under law.

Printed by CreateSpace, an Amazon.com Company
Available from Amazon.com and other retail outlets
www.CreateSpace.com/5759232

ISBN 978-3-00-051283-4

Visit Michael Kraft online at: **www.michaelkraft.net**

TABLE OF CONTENTS

Glossary of Terms	4
About the Author	5
Introduction	6
The Harmonic Series	9

SCALES

Chapter 1: First Position – Frets 2 - 5	15
Chapter 2: Second Position – Frets 5 - 8	37
Chapter 3: Third Position – Frets 9 - 12	59

CHORDS

Chapter 1: First Position – Frets 2 - 5	81
Chapter 2: Second Position – Frets 5 - 8	91
Chapter 3: Third Position – Frets 9 - 12	97

ETUDES

Chapter 1: First Position	105
Chapter 2: Second Position	111
Chapter 3: Third Position	117

Conclusion	123
Blank Charts	125

Glossary of Terms

fundamental: the lowest pitch of a musical note. The fundamental is also consider a harmonic!

harmonic: any member of the harmonic series, the set of frequencies that are multiples of the fundamental.

harmonic series: a group of frequencies that are multiples of the fundamental.

multiphonic: is an extended technique on a musical instrument that normally generates one note at a time, in which multiple tones are produced simultaneously. Not to be confused with a chord!

overtone: a synonym for harmonic. Please be aware that it refers to all harmonics *except* for the fundamental!

partial: refers to any of the sine waves that make up a tone. For our purposes, it is used as a synonym for *harmonic*.

timbre: is what distinguishes one musical sound from another (e.g. why a bass sounds different than a tuba).

About the Author

Author, bassist, composer and educator Michael Kraft holds a Master's degree in Jazz Composition from the Swiss Jazz School, a Master's in Jazz Performance from the State University of Performing Arts in Stuttgart, Germany and a Bachelor of Science in Music Business from Middle Tennessee State University. Notable teachers included Gerry Hemingway, Django Bates, Frank Sikora, Klaus König, Heiri Känzig and Dr. Edward Rainbow.

His 2007 debut CD for the *Neuklang* record label featured Grammy – nominated pianist Dana Landry and Argentinean drummer Daniel Messina. His big band compositions have been recorded by the Lucerne School of Music in Switzerland. Upcoming projects include: *Michael Kraft's Aural Canvas: de Jong's Universe,* featuring tone-poems for large jazz ensemble written to the paintings of Guy de Jong, *Odd Times* for jazz quartet, and a three – volume method book entitled *Odd Meters for the Improvising Musician.*

For more information, please visit **www.michaelkraft.net**

Introduction

How does one learn a language? The majority of us begin with the alphabet, move on to words/vocabulary, proceed to learn the rules of grammar, listen and observe people communicating, practice writing and progress to conversation and/or speech. Learning music, itself a form of communication, is no different. We learn the 12 tones available to us in our well-tempered system, become familiar with the modes, harmony and rhythm (vocabulary), move on to voice leading, resolution, and the rules of parallel motion (grammar), listen to and study historically significant recordings, compose, practice, and ultimately rehearse and perform with others (conversation).

This book presents material in a similar way, beginning with an introduction to the Harmonic Series, followed by the presentation of scales and chords, and ending with exercises that utilize all of the material discussed in the previous chapters.

Using the standard one-finger-per-fret technique that you should all be familiar with, I have created three 'Positions', ranging from the 2nd to the 12th frets. The 1st Position includes frets 2 - 5, the 2nd Position also includes fret 5, along with 6 - 8. Redundant? Perhaps. But it will also help you to quickly commit this important fret to memory! Finally, frets 9 - 12 round out the 3rd Position. The Scales, Arpeggios, Chords and Études all abide strictly to these Positions.

Noticeably absent is the remainder of the fingerboard. I made a conscious to omit anything beyond the 12th fret because:

1. Unlike fretted, or stopped notes, the harmonics in the upper register are in the same octave as their counterparts located on the bottom half of the fretboard.
2. Using the octave (12th fret) harmonic as an axis, the location of harmonics in either direction is symmetrical.
3. There are actually fewer possibilities beyond the 12th fret. Those in the upper part of the Harmonic Series are very close together, and because the frets beyond the 12th fret are smaller, they are nearly impossible to reproduce, especially for those with large fingers.
4. When it comes to the number of frets, there is no standard. Some of you may have 20 frets, others 21, and some 24 or more.

All of these factors made it redundant and/or unnecessary to discuss harmonics beyond the 12th fret.

Tablature has been deliberately avoided. There are no shortcuts in life or music. That being said, the notation, developed by American composer Elliott Carter, *is* actually a form of tablature! The bottom note always shows the open string, the diamond - headed note head shows the location on the fretboard (tab), and the uppermost note (enclosed in parentheses), shows the sounding pitch. This ingenious form of notation eliminates the confusion that may arise from alternative forms of harmonic notation.

Theoretically, harmonics that are out of tune should be notated accordingly. I decided against using this notation, as it is primarily used in contemporary classical music and the electric bass is generally ignored and/or marginalized in the classical community. It also adds clutter to the written page, especially when dealing with triplets or shorter note values. Reading the material will already be a challenge for most, so I avoided using this notation altogether. In order for you to get acquainted with harmonic notation, I've included an example of it along with each scale.

The purpose of this book is not to present every scale known to man. I specifically focused on the scales that any serious musician should be familiar with – the Church Modes and the most important modes of the Harmonic and Melodic Minor scales. The last 2 pages in the book contain Blank Charts that can be copied so the student can notate exotic scales and chords that haven't been discussed in the text. This also follows my pedagogical philosophy that some of the effort must come from the student.

In creating the scales, I was least concerned with creating step-wise, ascending motion and more concerned with maintaining sound continuity and an economy of motion (avoiding and/or limiting large string skips). Let me explain the concept of sound continuity. Aside from the fact that some overtones are more out-of-tune than others, some sound much different than others. Some, especially the major triads of each open string, sound much fuller or even louder than those higher up in the harmonic series. The 7ths, Major 9ths, Major 10ths and the 3rd octave are much more fragile compared to their counterparts found lower in the harmonic series.

Just as it is important in composing with and/or using Slash Chords to avoid a patchwork collection of slash chords, triads and 7th chords, so is it necessary to create and/or maintain an environment with similar sounding harmonics. In composing the Etudes, I adhered strictly to the confines of the positions that I established. This was done in order for the student to gain maximum familiarity of the harmonics in a specific area of the neck. At times, the inclusion of 'clashing' harmonics was unavoidable. The experienced musician will recognize this immediately. Nevertheless, it does not diminish the effectiveness of the Etudes.

Unlike the more popular extended techniques of slapping and tapping, harmonics are not largely dependent on technique. There are, however, a few things that will make reproducing overtones less difficult. Your instrument, specifically the materials that were used to construct your instrument, will make your life easier, or more of a challenge.

The features that have an important impact on harmonics are:

- **Fingerboard** – a maple or phenolic/graphite/composite fingerboard will yield the best results. These materials have better definition, attack and evenness in sound. This doesn't mean that you should buy a new instrument or give up your quest to learn the material. Jaco Pastorious and Victor Wooten rarely perform(ed) on maple and/or graphite fingerboards and they are pioneers in the art of harmonics!
- **Strings** – generally the lighter & brighter, the better. You'll have to experiment to determine which give you the best results. This may involve sacrificing your personal preference to those strings that best suit your instrument!
- **Electronics** – modern pickups will best reproduce the harmonics on your instrument. Regardless of your personal preference (vintage, tube, etc...), modern electronics are far more advanced and accurate than those from the past.

Upon completion of this book, the student should be comfortable incorporating harmonics into their playing. They should also be able to transfer their knowledge to extended range basses, utilize harmonics in alternate tunings, and improvise or compose using them.

Now it's time to begin our study of *Harmonics for the Bass Guitarist & Contemporary Composer*.

The Harmonic Series
A Brief Overview

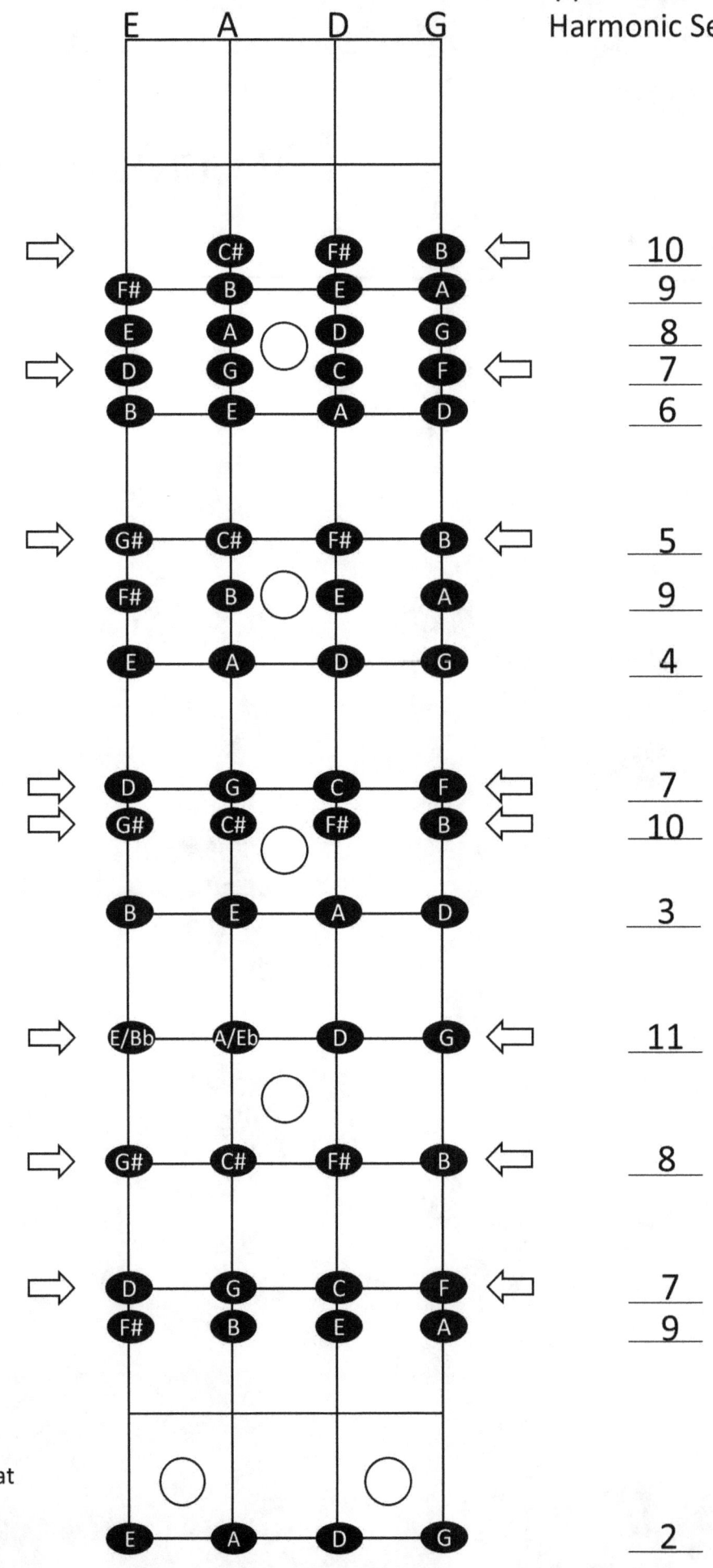

G String

D String

A String

E String

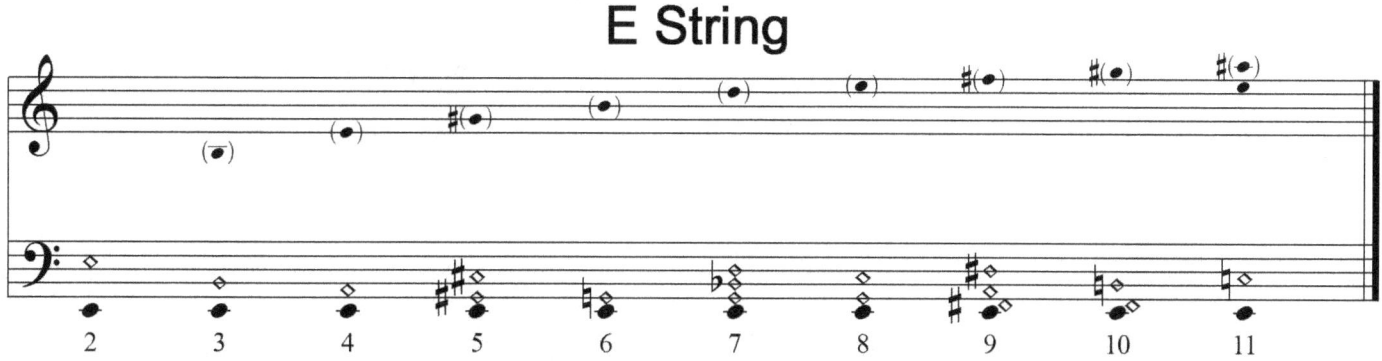

I was first exposed to the *harmonic series* as an undergraduate jazz studies major at The University of North Texas. It showed up again in my curriculum as a Recording Industry major at Middle Tennessee State University. Later, as a Master's student, I was confronted with the topic once again. First, in the form of the contemporary classical composition *Die Rose,* by the young English composer Sophie Pope, and finally as part of my studies as a composition student in Lucerne, Switzerland.

I left the initial lectures feeling frustrated and bewildered. The topic was being taught from a Physicist's perspective. I had no connection whatsoever to the material. It felt like it was just another requirement to fulfill and I was just 'going through the motions.' Later in my studies I finally learned what it meant to me, the *musician*.

The following pages present a straightforward, streamlined summary of the harmonic series. Those wishing to delve further into the topic will find ample material available.

The *harmonic series* is a naturally occurring phenomenon that is responsible for the *timbre* of an instrument, or how it sounds, as well as the location of *harmonics* on our instrument. Other factors play a role in creating the *timbre* of an instrument, but the strength of specific *harmonics* are a vital piece of the puzzle.

In our haste as musicians/composers to be praised by superlatives, we often overlook, forget or completely ignore the more subtle elements of our craft. Many become so enveloped in being the fastest, loudest, or most innovative, that they take these subtleties for granted.

Try this simple, yet effective exercise to raise your awareness to the delicate nuances of sound:

Go to your practice room. Plug in your instrument. For maximum concentration, turn off the lights. We want to block out anything that may interfere with your concentration. Pluck a note, any note. Let it ring for its entire duration. What do you hear (aside from the *fundamental*)?

Each note is perceived as one sound, when, in fact, it consists of many individual parts. For our intents and purposes, the individual parts are *harmonics*. Try it again. Can you hear the octave? Perhaps a 5th? Maybe even a Major 3rd?

Now refer to the chart on page 12 which maps out harmonics between the 2nd and 12th frets, as well as the following page, which notates each of the harmonics shown. It's time to demystify the subject matter once and for all!

We will refer to the open string as the *fundamental*, or lowest frequency. The fundamental is also considered the 1st harmonic. A *harmonic* is any member of the *harmonic series*. Harmonics are also referred to as *partials* and *overtones*. Use care in using the latter as a substitute, however. Overtones refer to all harmonics *except for* the fundamental!

If you look closely, you will see that each string yields a dominant 9th chord, albeit not in the typical interval of a third that we are accustomed to. Also notice that all tones except for Bb and Eb are represented (they do, however, appear as *multiphonics/Mehrklänge*).

The 2nd harmonic yields the octave. It divides the string in half and is located on the 12th fret. The 3rd harmonic is located an octave and a Perfect 5th above the fundamental. The 4th partial is two octaves above the fundamental. The 5th is a Major Third, which also happens to be very flat (in pitch). The 6th is another Perfect 5th, an octave above the initial occurrence. The 7th yields a minor 7th, even more out of tune than the Major Third. Don't take my word for it – check it out yourself! Fret an 'F' on the D string and compare it to any of the 'F' harmonics on the G String. You don't have to be a trained musician to recognize that it's almost a quarter tone out of tune!

The 8th partial is, conveniently, yet another octave above the fundamental. The 9th gives us a Major 9th, the 10th a (flat) Major 10th, and the 11th a Tritone. Not everyone will be capable of reproducing harmonics 9 – 11. The construction of your instrument will play a role in your ability to sound the upper partials (see the Introduction for a more detailed explanation).

In my more than twenty years of studying, performing and teaching music, I have yet to come across a bassist that thinks in terms of the harmonic series to locate harmonics on the fretboard. We spend so many years memorizing our fingerboard so we can effortlessly navigate around it that it is easier for us to relate harmonics to what we already know. I'm sure there are those of you that may think in terms of string length and/or the harmonic series, and that's great! Variety is the spice of life! There is no *right way* to integrate this material into your playing. There is just *YOUR WAY!*

Let me share this profound musical experience with you…

I had the privilege of attending a Master Class of the late, great pianist Kenny Drew, Jr. I greatly admired his music and playing, and knew he had a vast repertoire of tunes (also from classical and pop genres!) committed to memory.

The clinic was intended for pianists, but I prepared some general questions to ask him. The main question that I asked was how he went about memorizing so many tunes. He must have a method, I thought. Perhaps he related songs to one another (e.g. these tunes begin with a II – V – I progression, the form of these tunes is identical, these songs share the same key, etc…). There are entire method books devoted to the topic, so I was certain he would share his 'secret.'

Imagine my surprise when Kenny said that he didn't adhere to one particular method of memorizing tunes! He very nonchalantly explained that sometimes you have to play a song over, and over, and over again until you 'hear' it, or your fingers 'do the talking' (muscle memory).

The moral of the story – *just do it*! Sit yourself down and devote your precious time to adding this extended technique to your musical vocabulary!

Scales: Chapter 1
1st Position: Frets 2 - 5

Practice Suggestions for Scales/Arpeggios

1. Scales ascending to the seventh. Repeat as necessary.
2. Scales ascending to the seventh, then descending back to the root. Repeat.
3. Ascending arpeggios. Repeat.
4. Ascending, then descending arpeggios. Repeat.
5. Ascending scale, descending arpeggio. Repeat.
6. Ascending arpeggio, descending scale. Repeat.

Please note that the enclosed numbers are scale degrees, not fingerings. The transparent circles make the seventh chord easily identifiable.

- Release the left finger immediately after plucking for best results.
- Pluck close to the bridge to let the high overtones reach their maximum potential.

*the arrows identify the harmonics that are flat in pitch

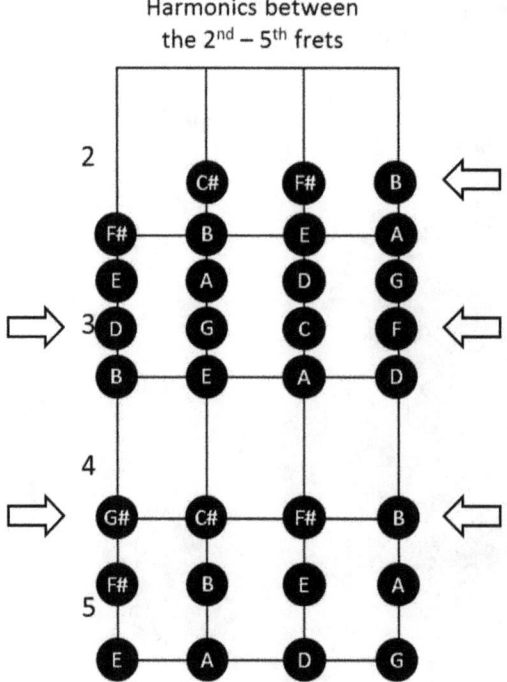

C Ionian

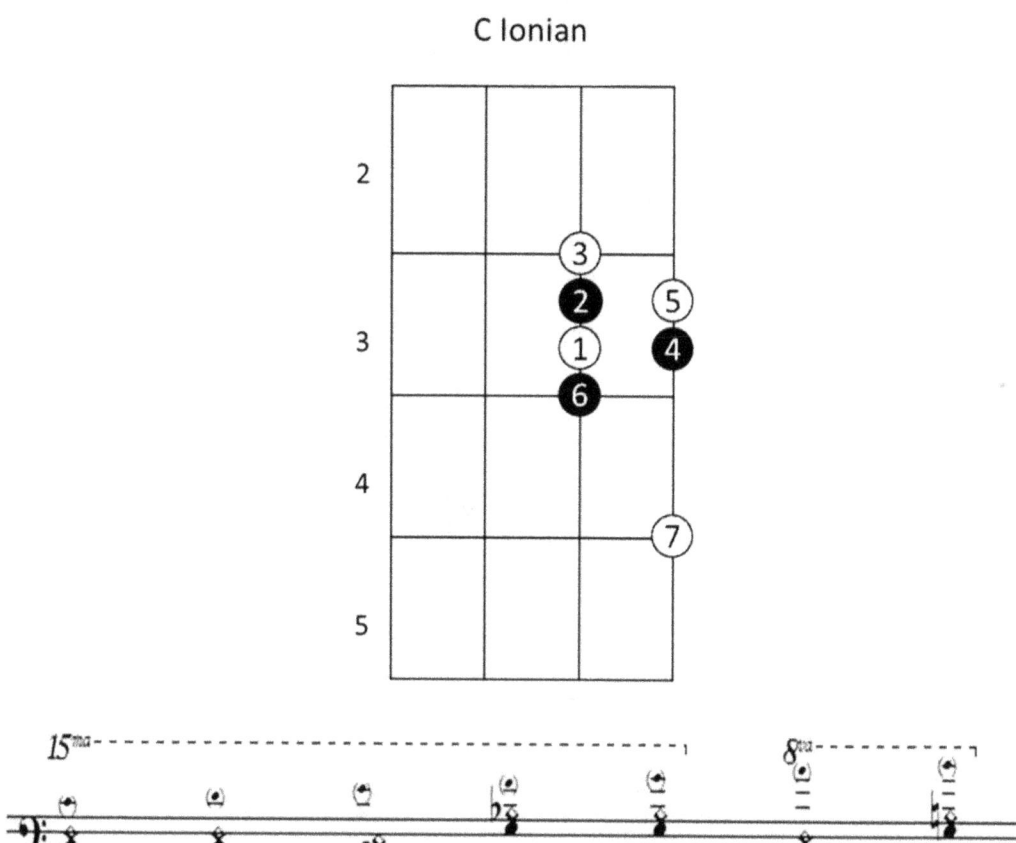

C Lydian

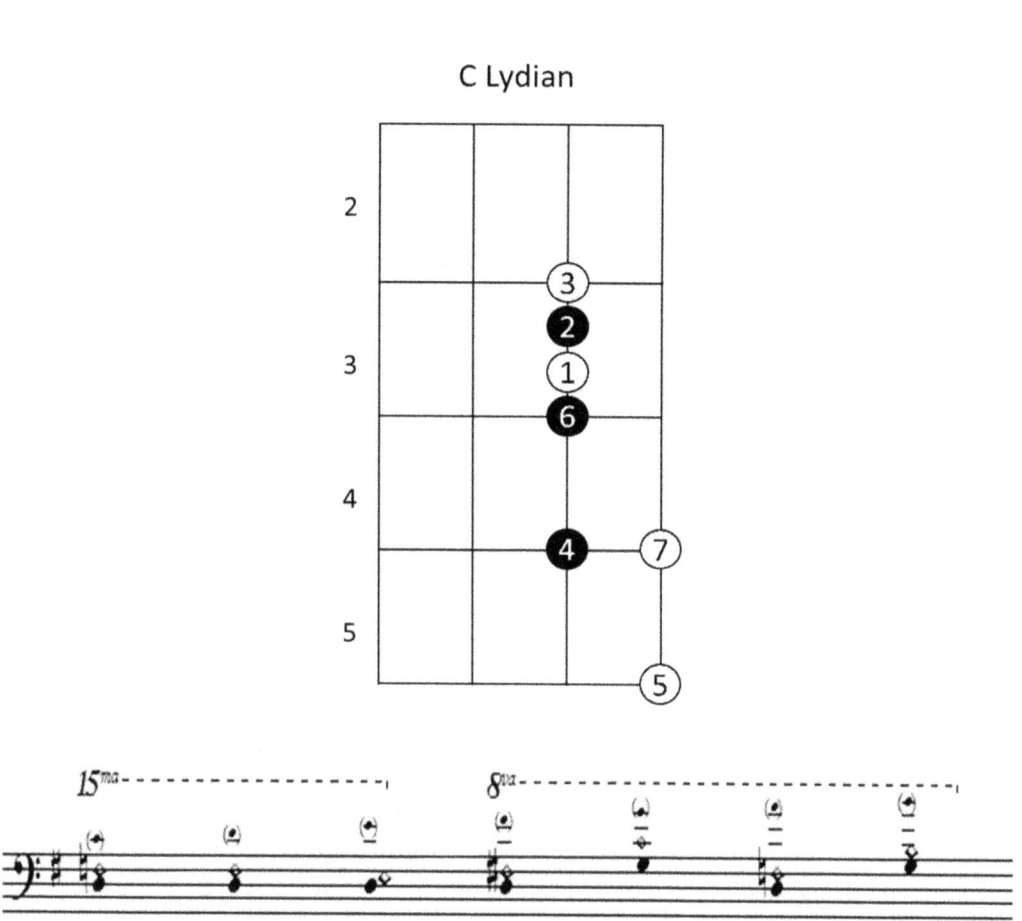

C# Locrian

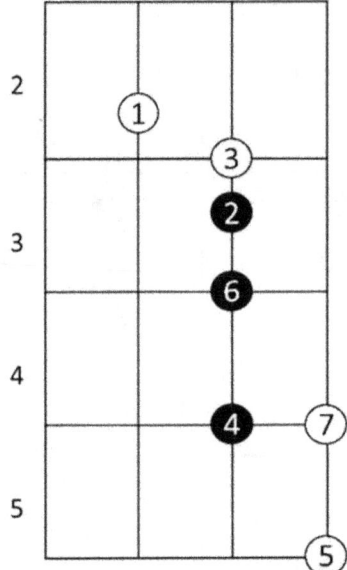

C# Altered

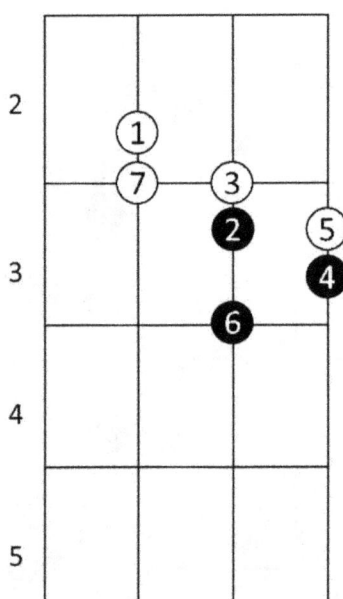

C# Phrygian

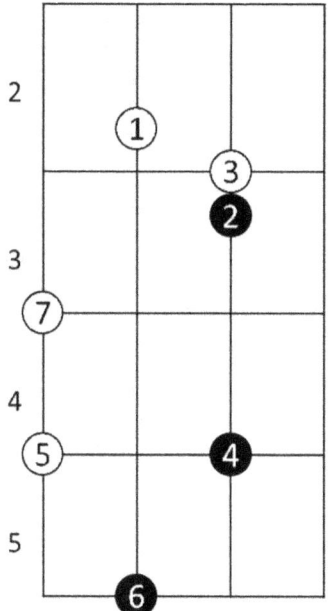

C# Mixo b9/b13

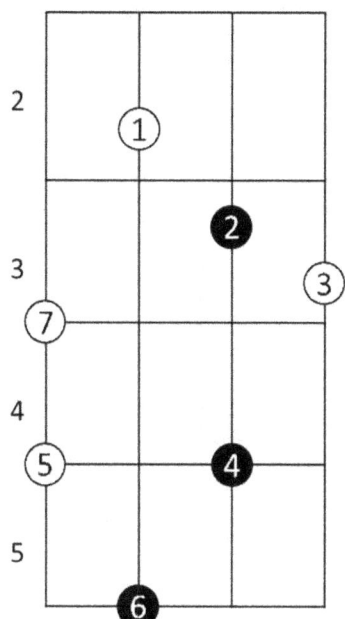

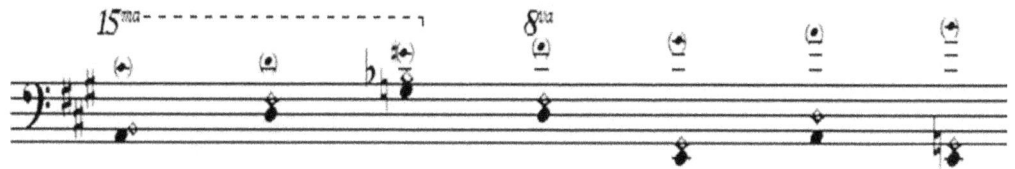

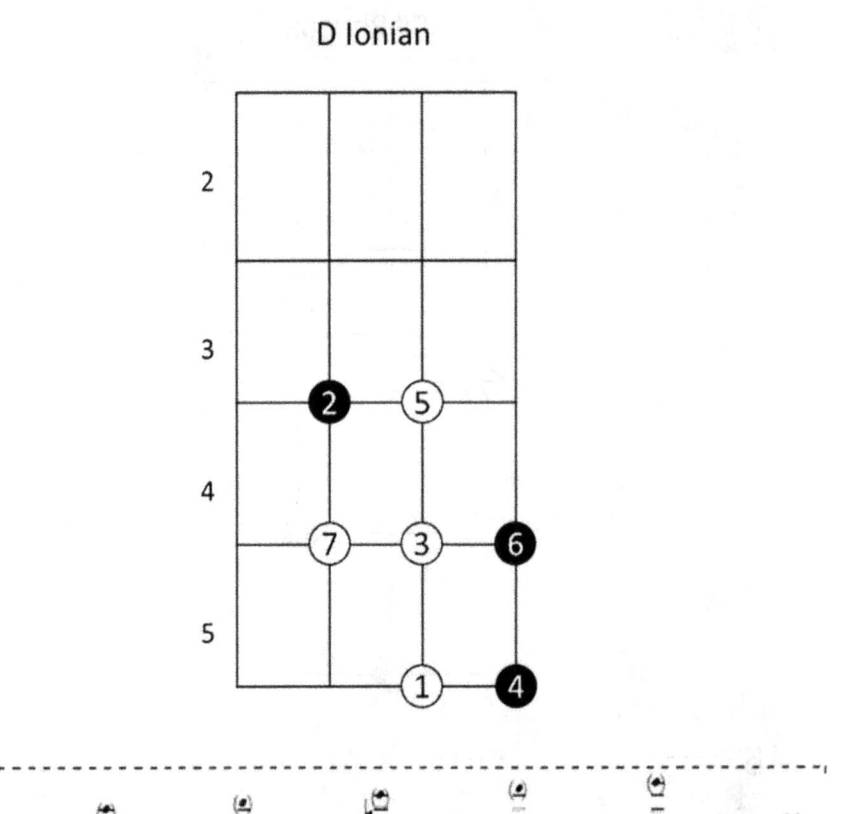

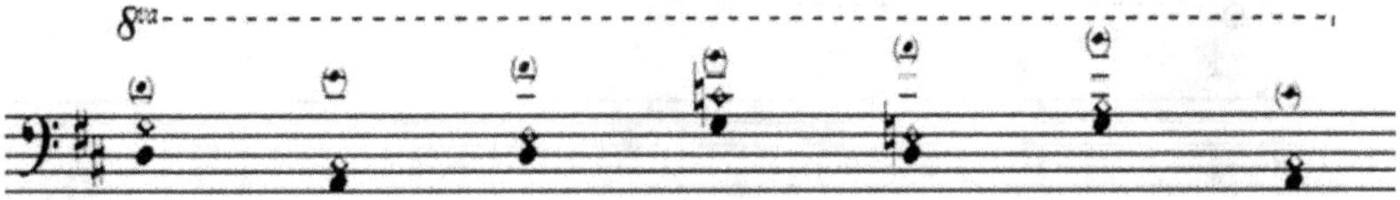

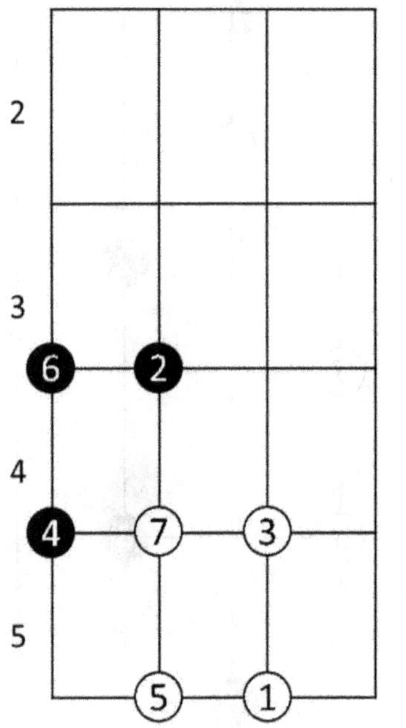

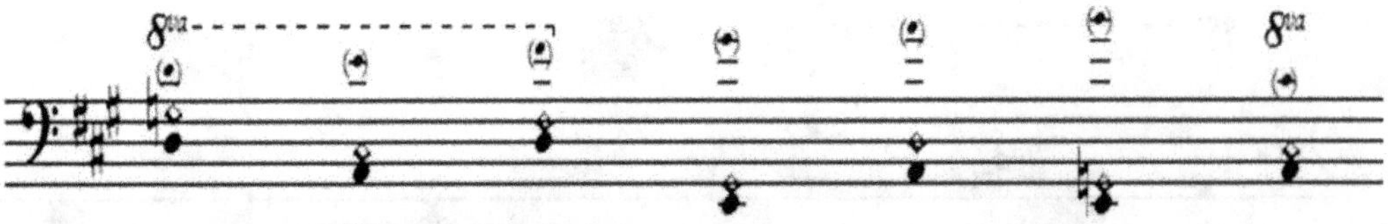

D Mixolydian

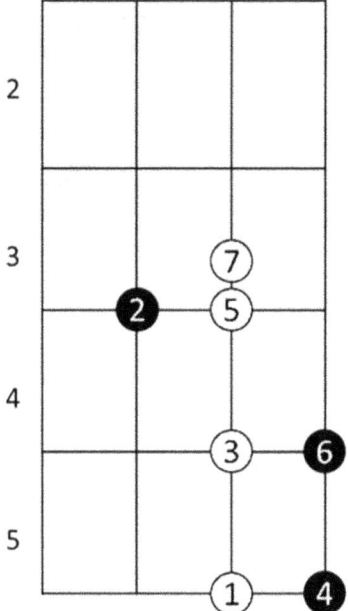

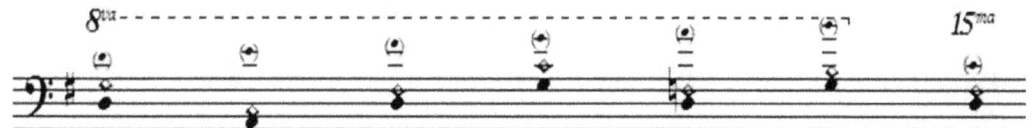

D Mixo #11

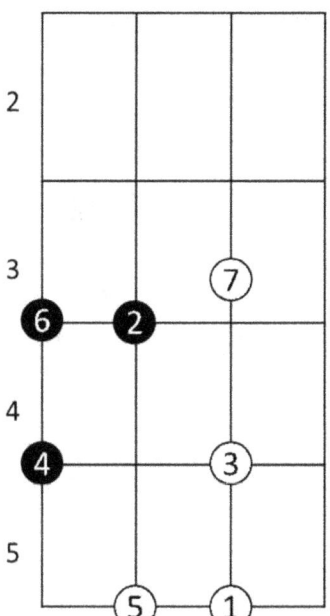

D Dorian

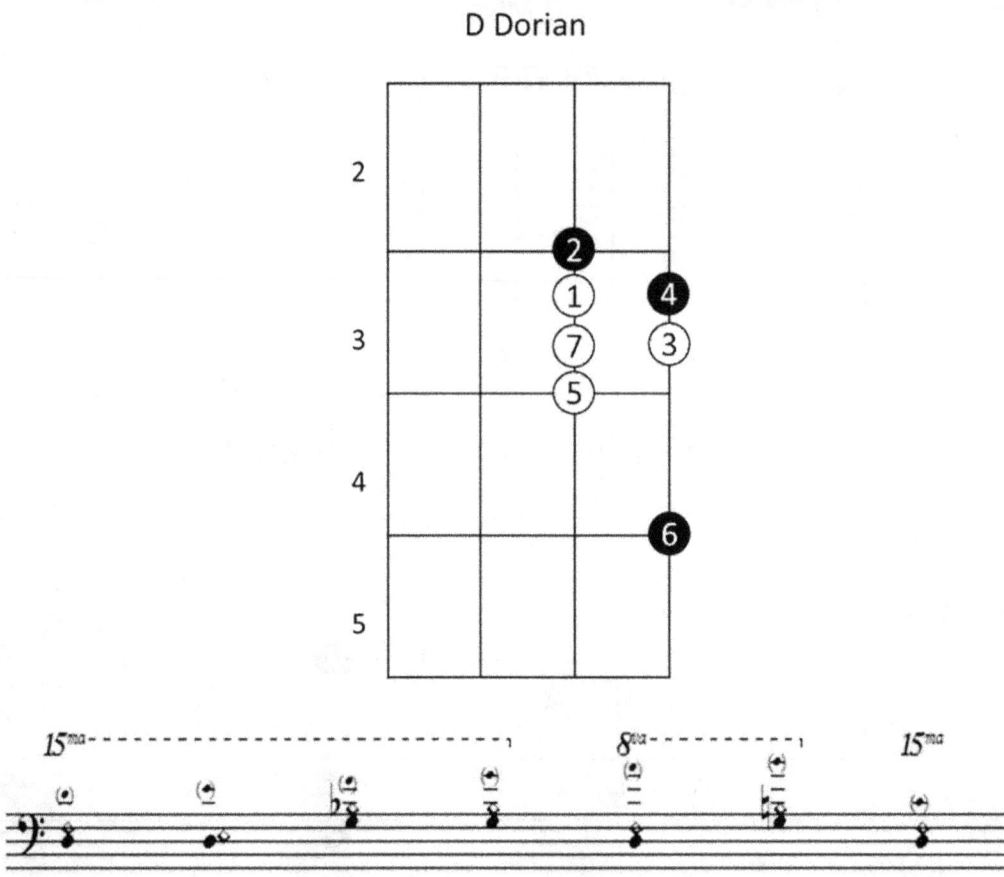

D Melodic Minor

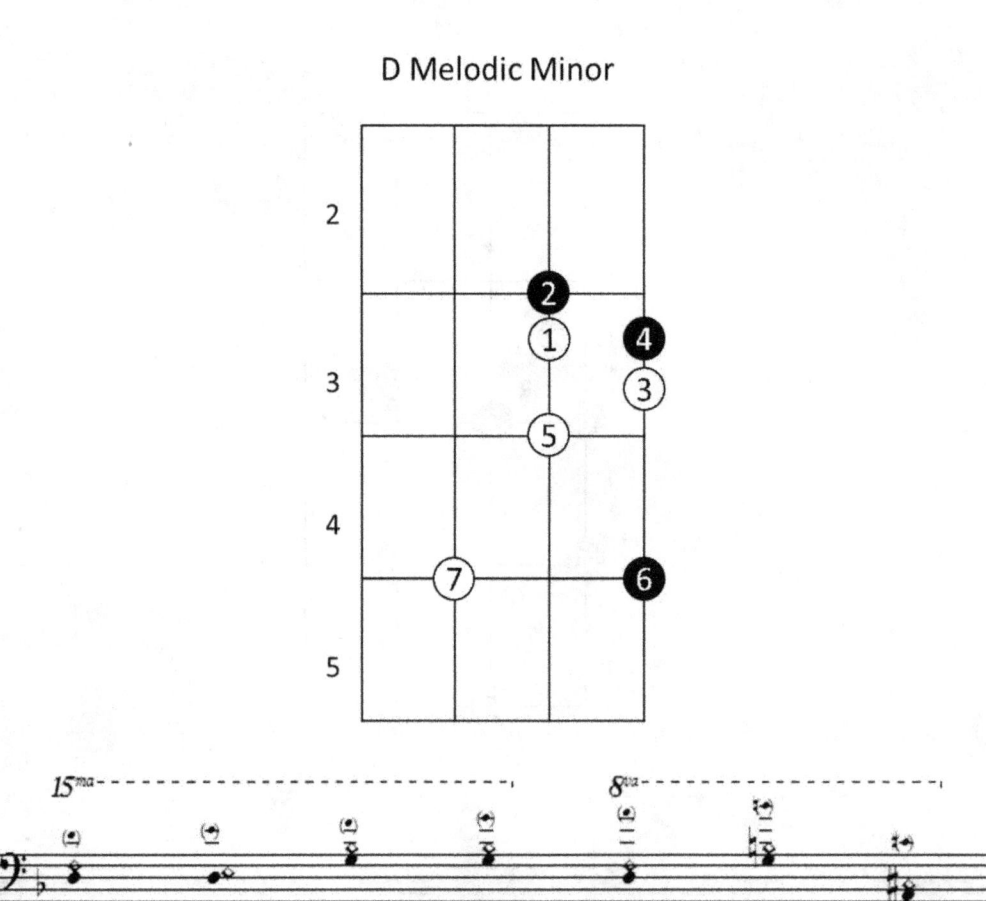

E Mixolydian

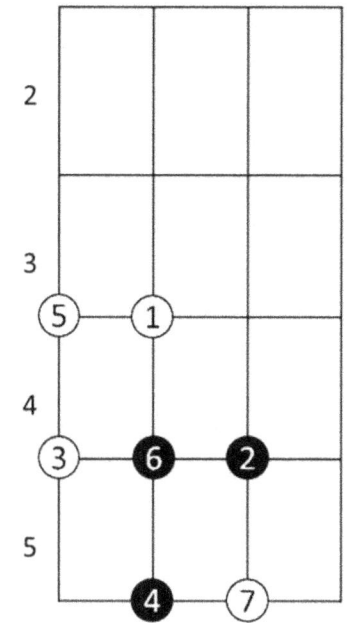

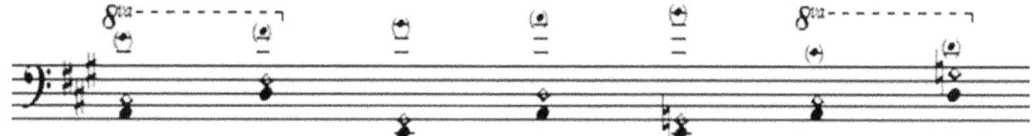

E Mixo b13

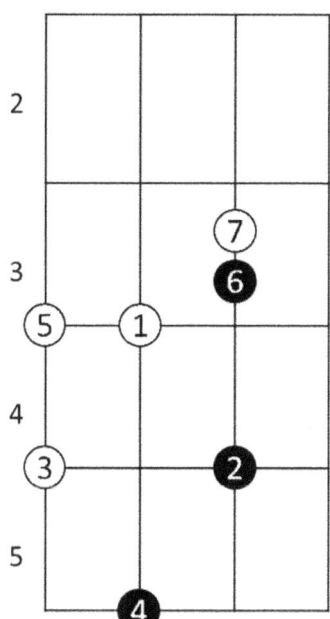

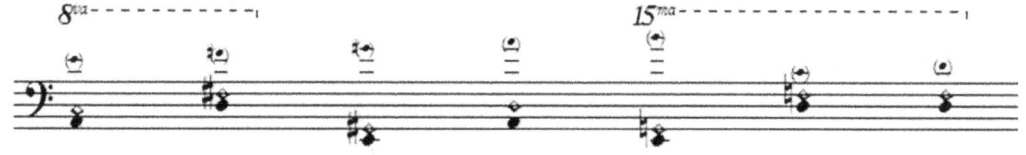

E Dorian

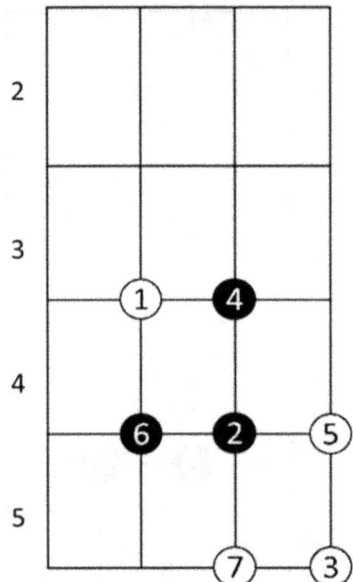

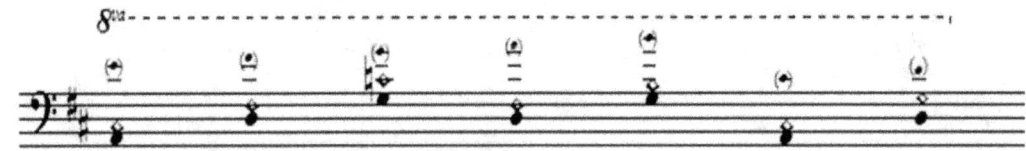

E Aeolian

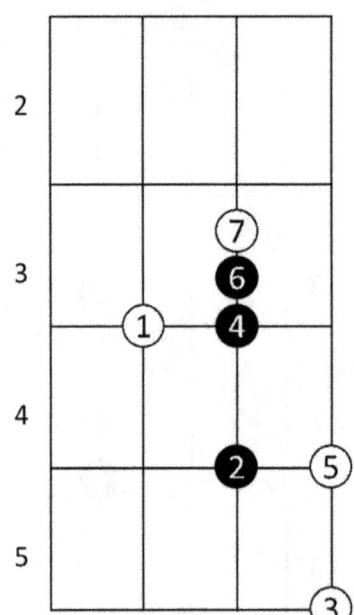

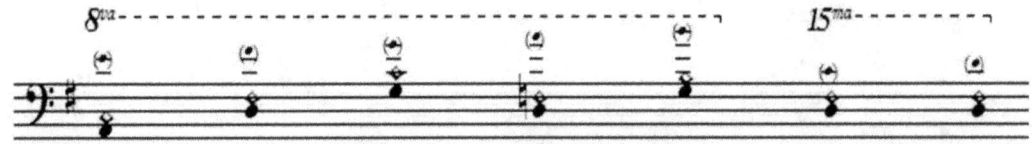

E Phrygian

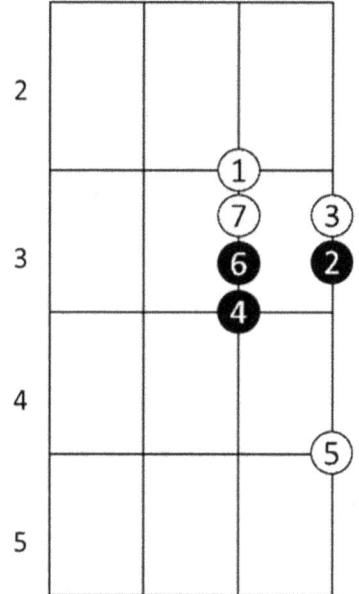
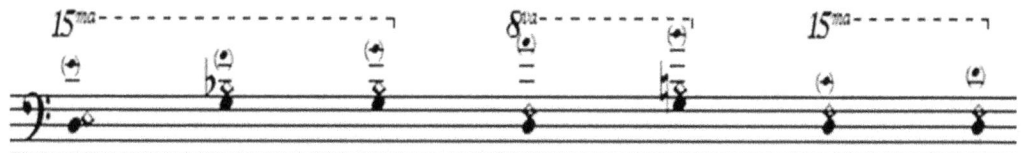

E Mixo b9/b13

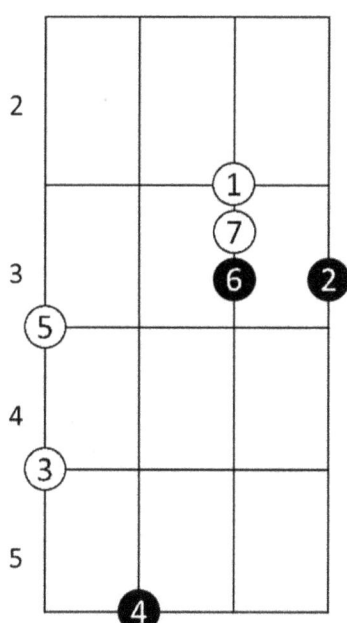
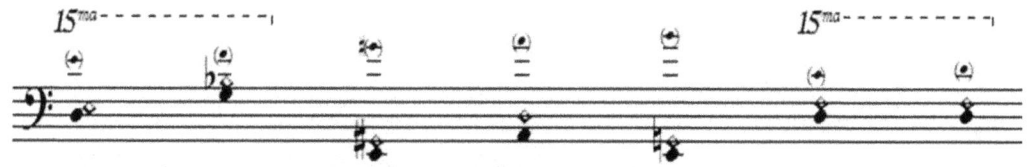

F Lydian

F# Aeolian

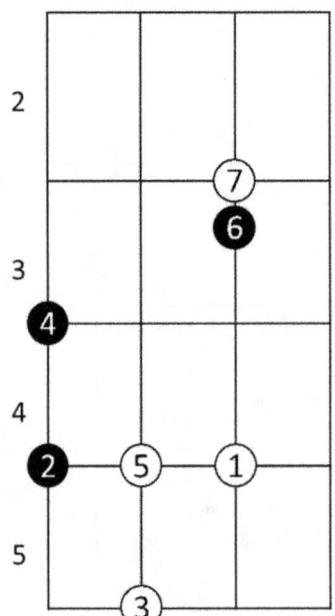

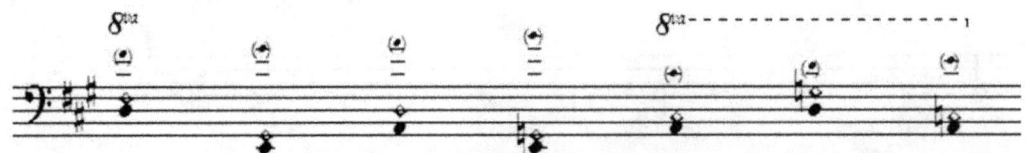

F# Harm Minor

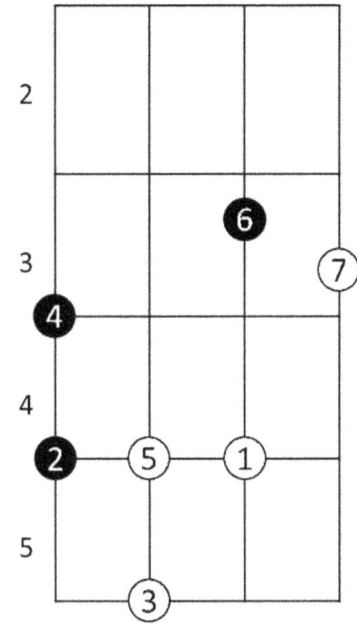

F# Phrygian

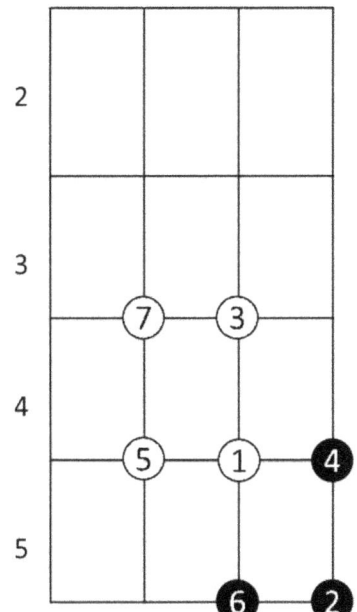

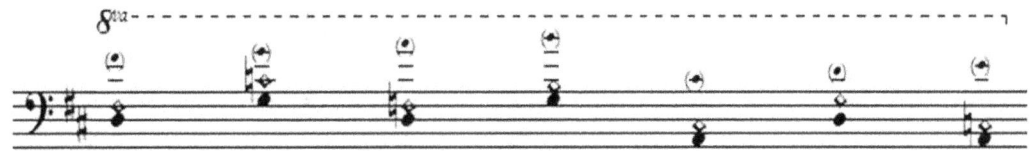

F# Locrian

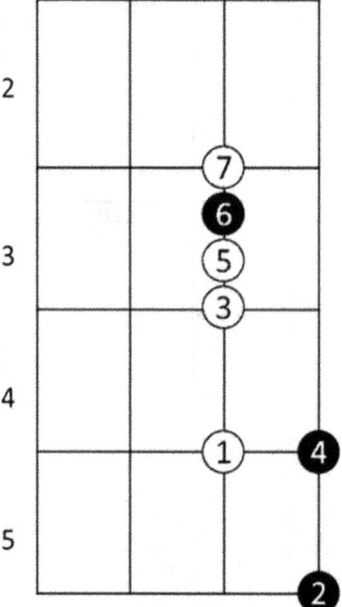

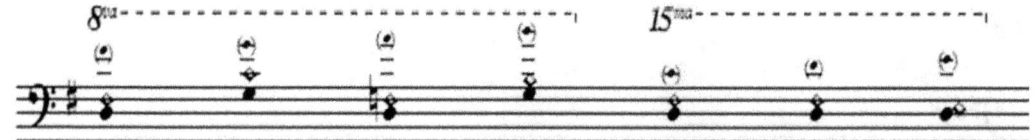

G Ionian

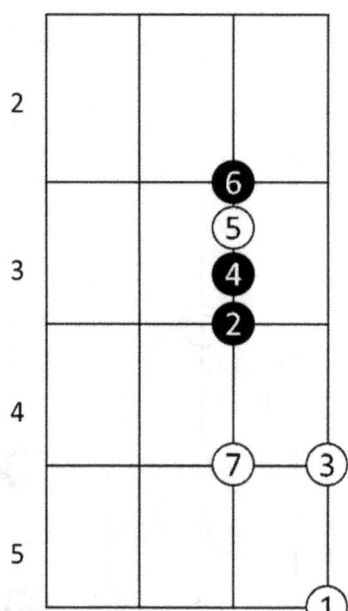

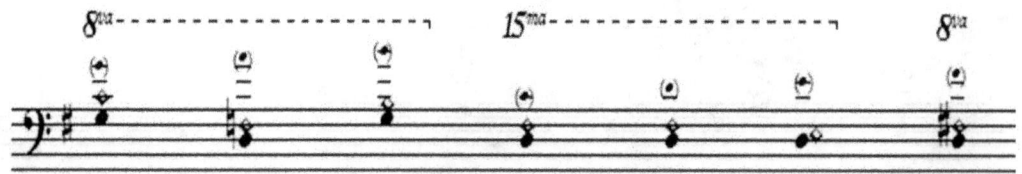

G Lydian

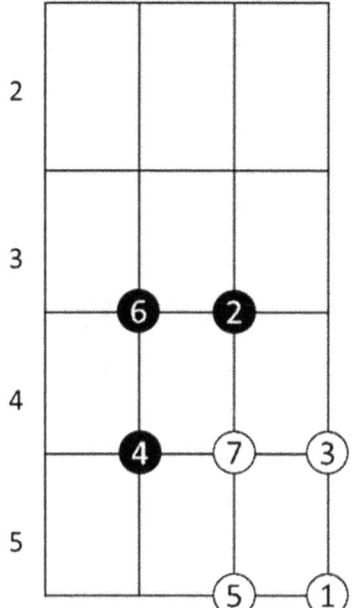

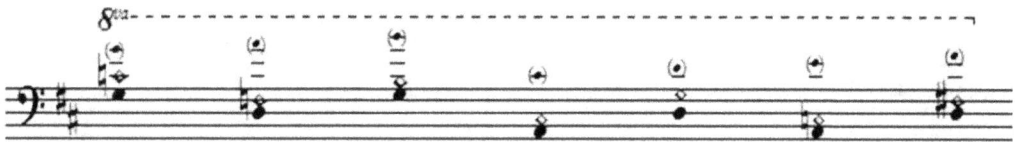

G Mixolydian

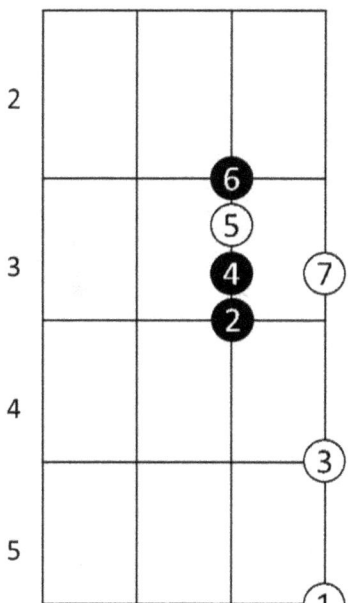

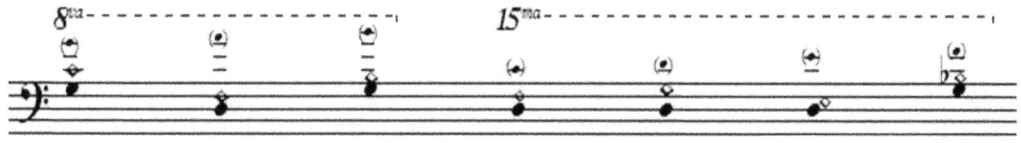

G Mixo #11

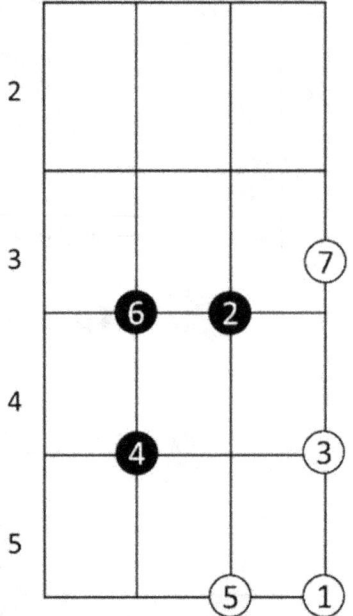

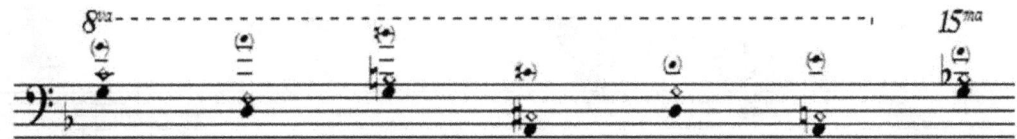

G# Altered

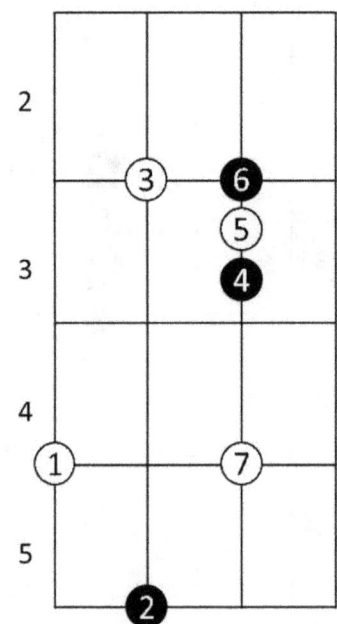

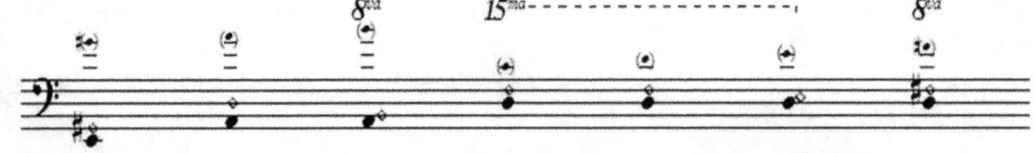

G# Locrian

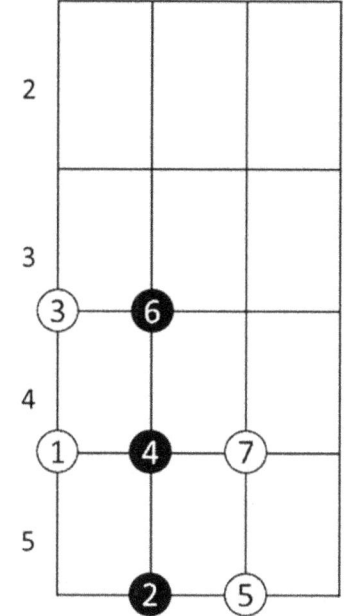

A Ionian

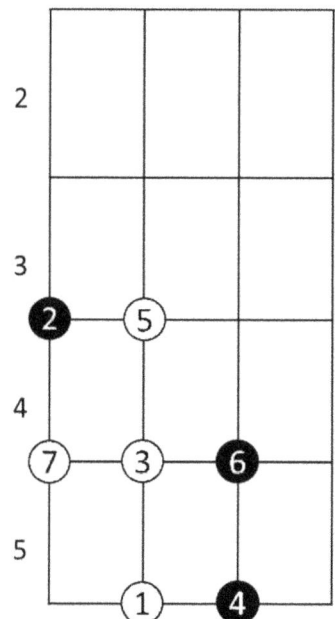

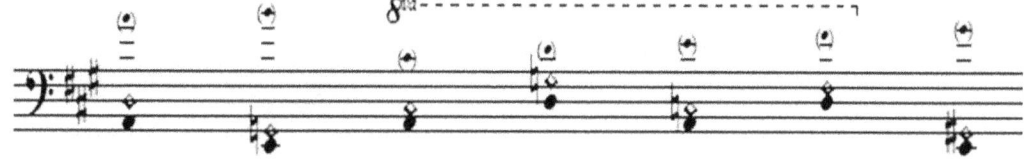

A Mixolydian

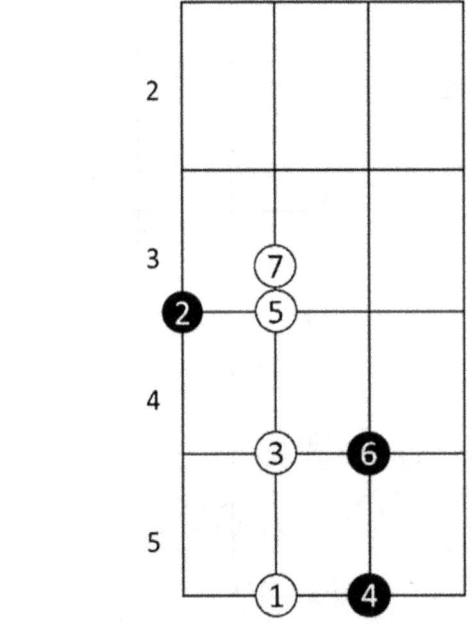

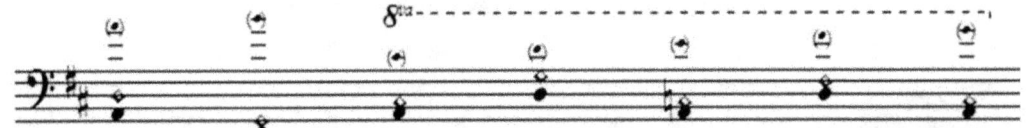

A Mixo b13

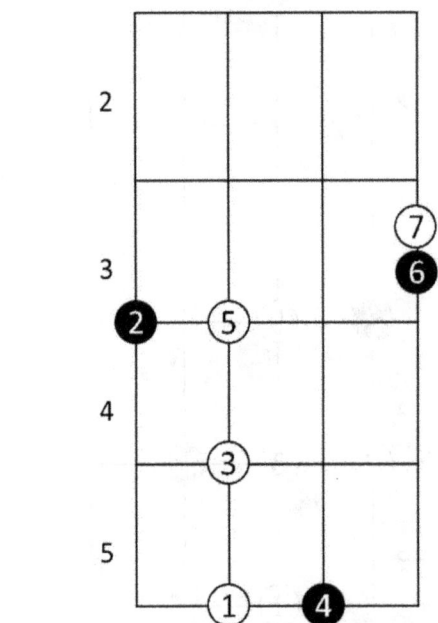

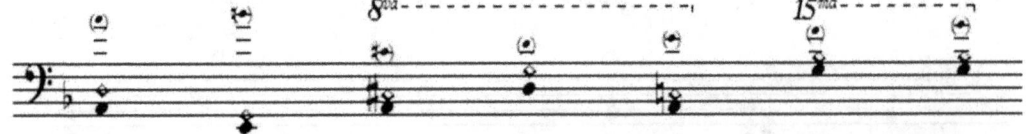

A Dorian

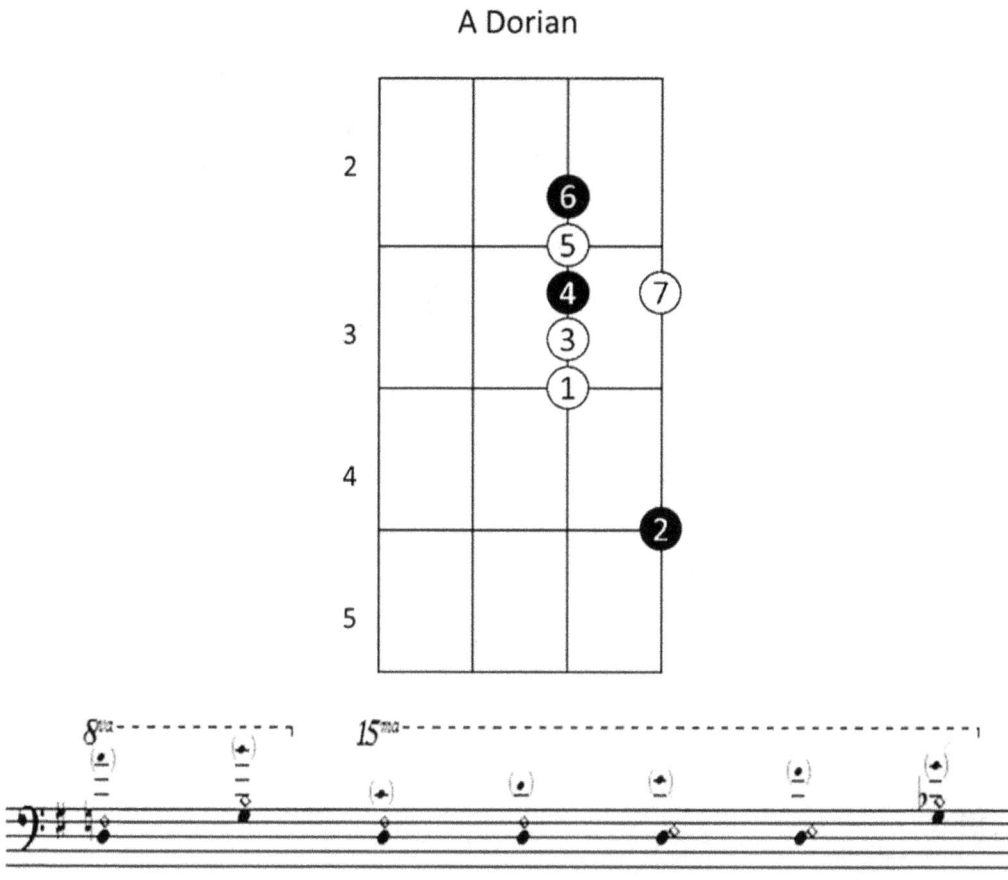

A Aeolian

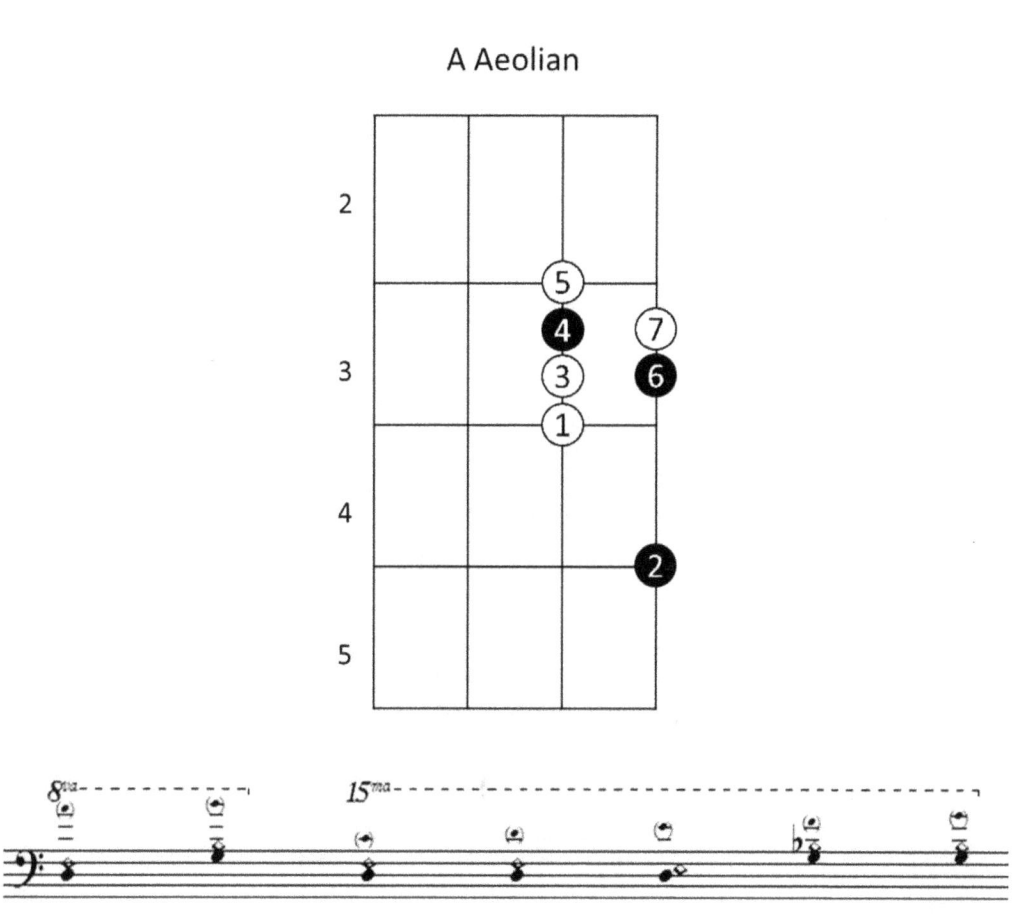

A Harm Minor

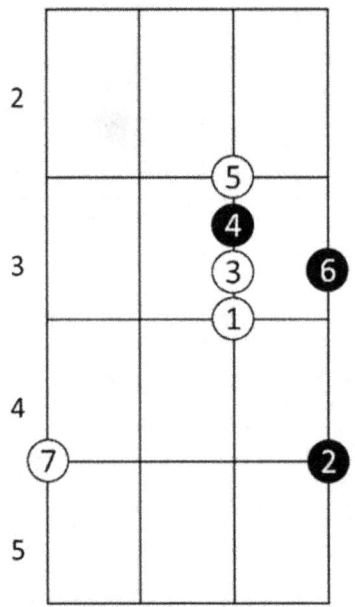

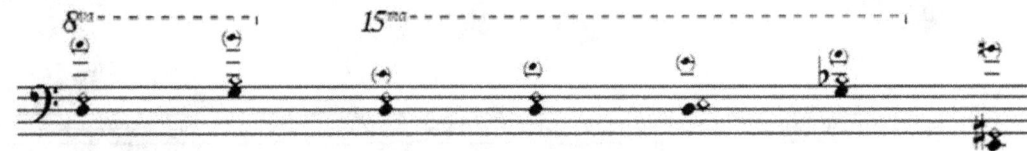

A Melodic Minor

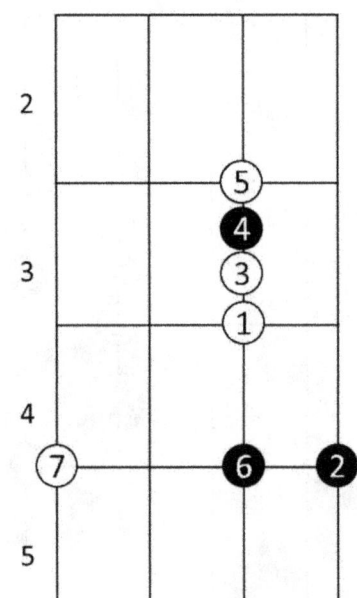

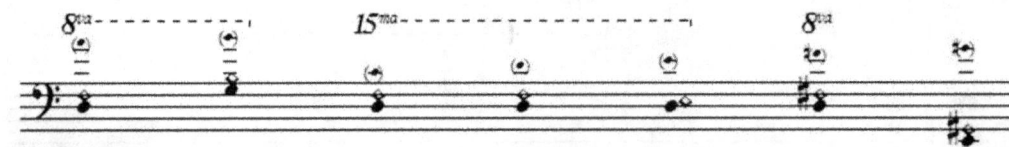

B Dorian

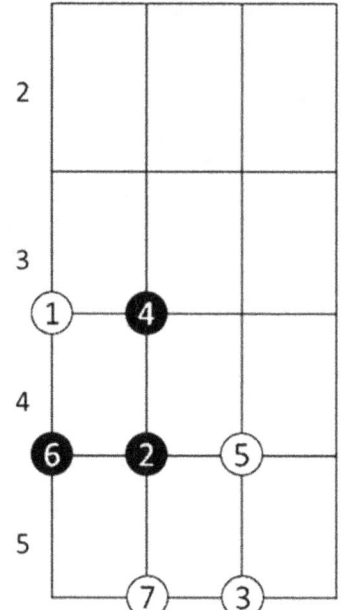

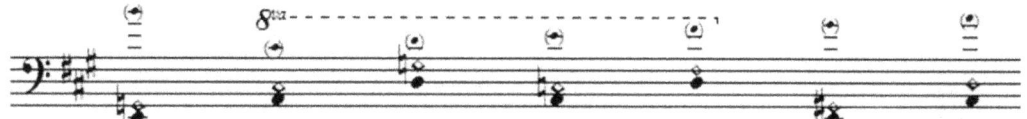

B Aeolian

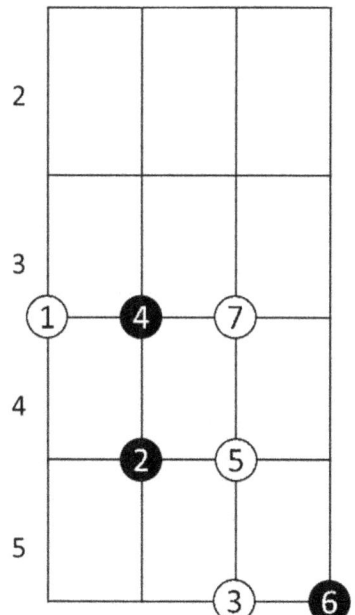

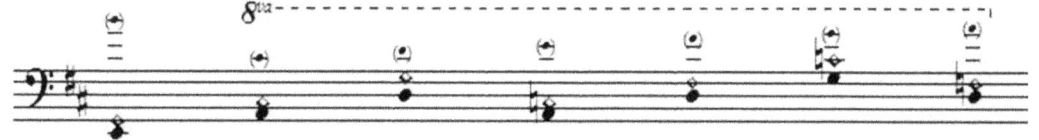

B Phrygian

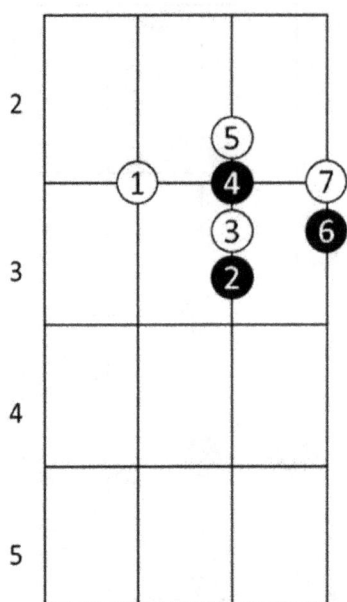

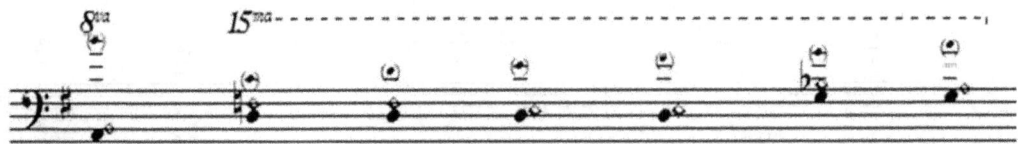

B Locrian

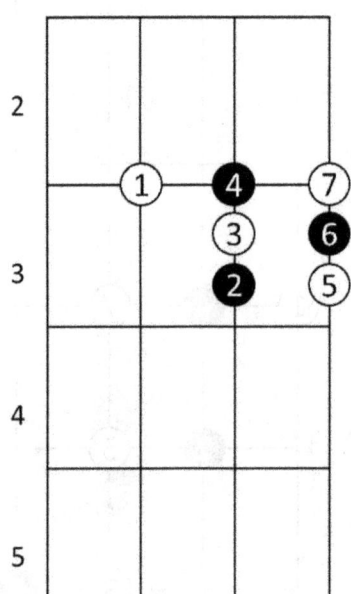

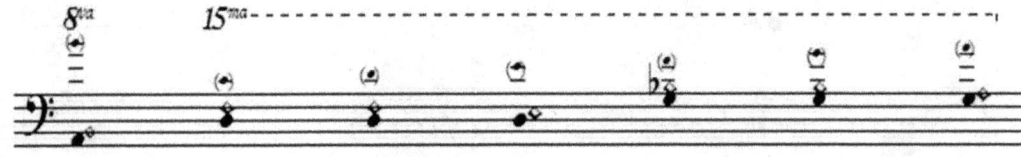

Scales: Chapter 2
2nd Position: Frets 5 - 8

Harmonics between the 5th – 8th frets

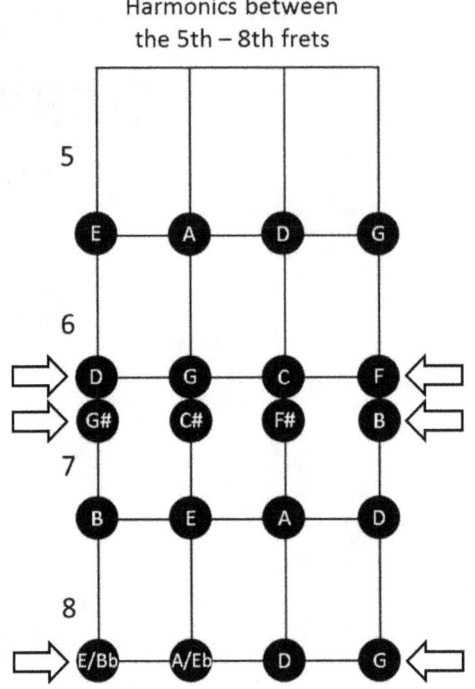

C Ionian

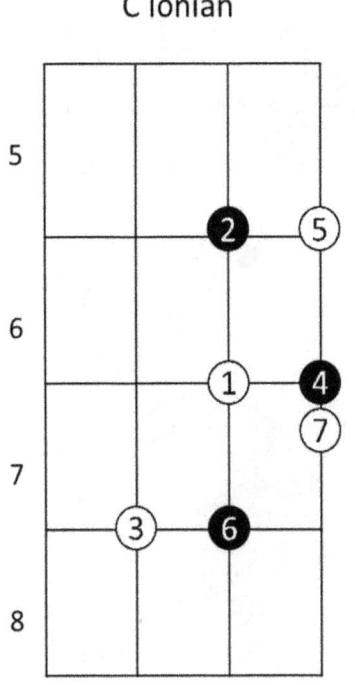

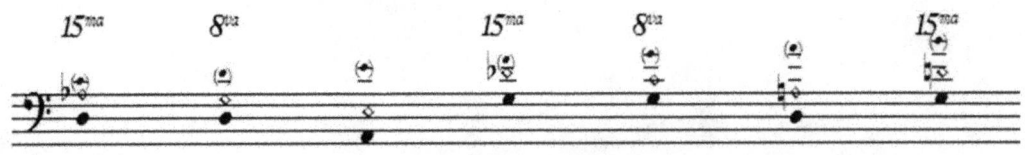

C Lydian

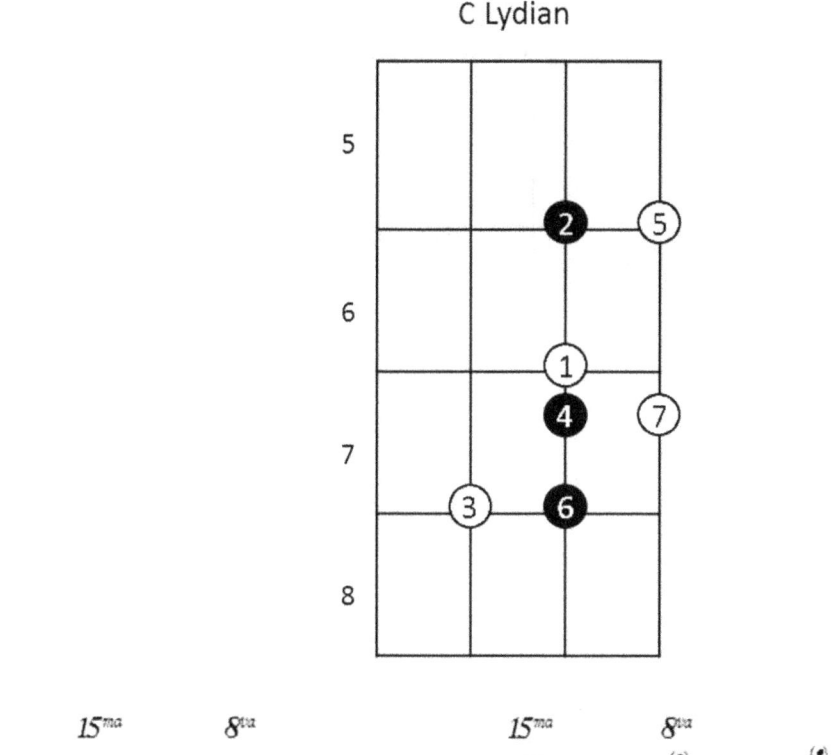

C# Mixo b9/b13

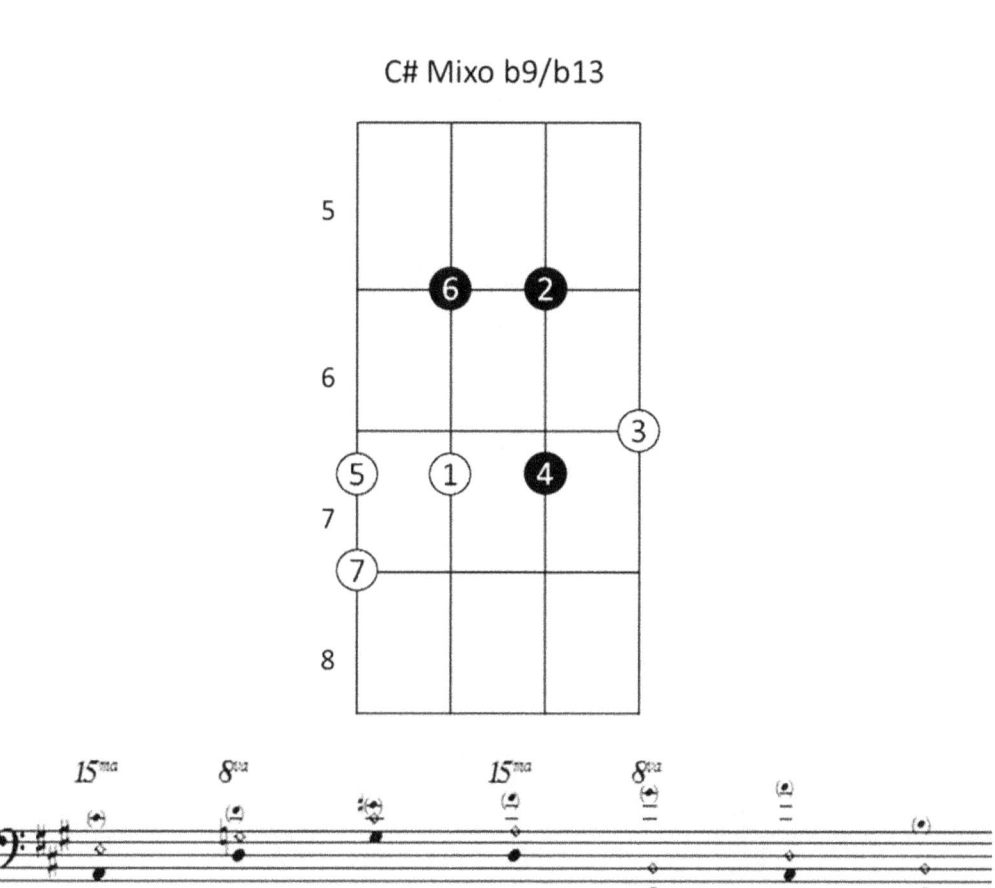

C# Altered

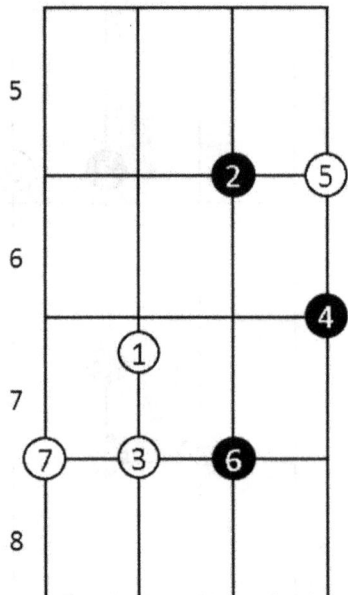

C# Phrygian

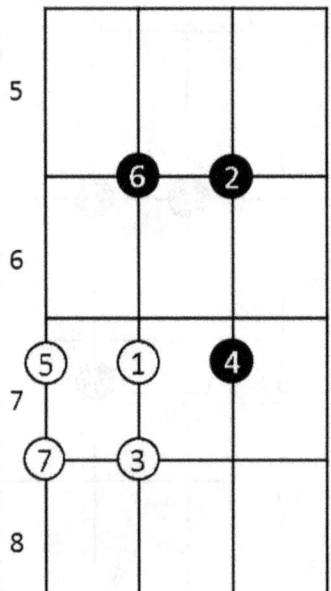

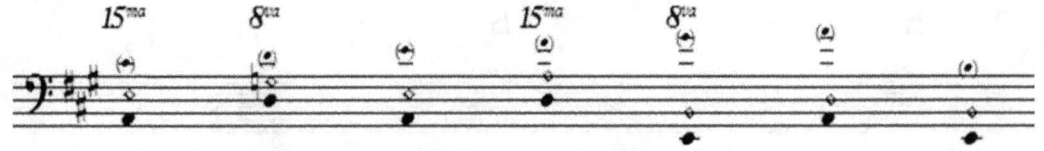

C# Locrian

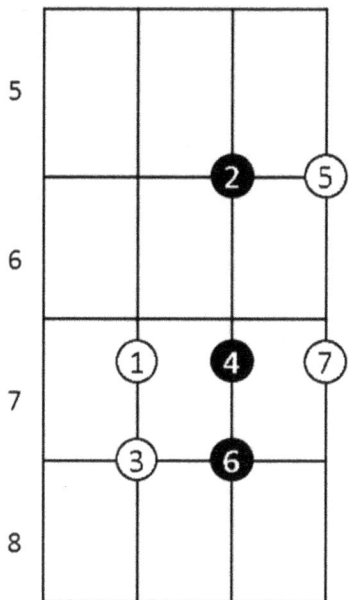

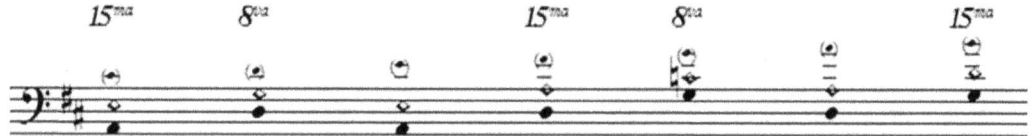

D Ionian

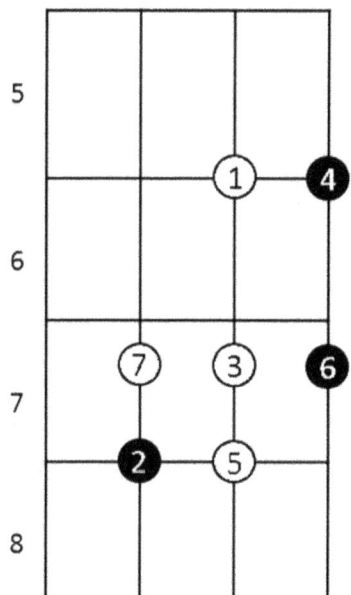

D Lydian

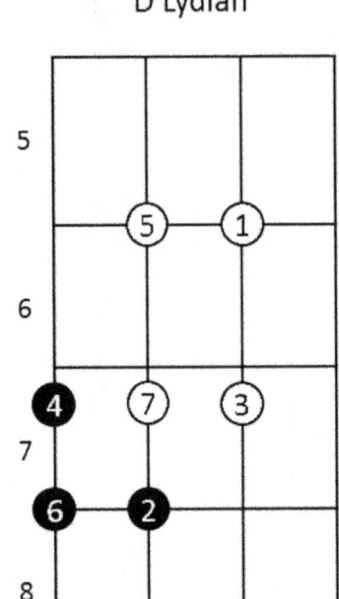

D Mixolydian

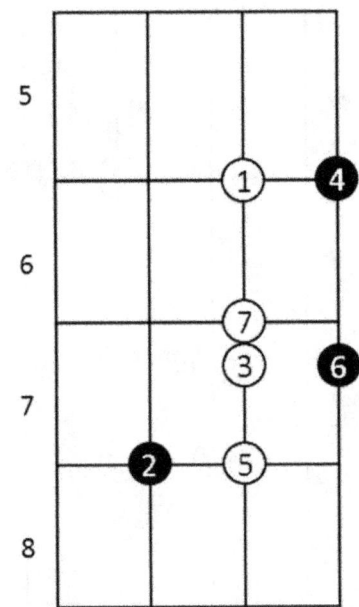

D Mixo #11

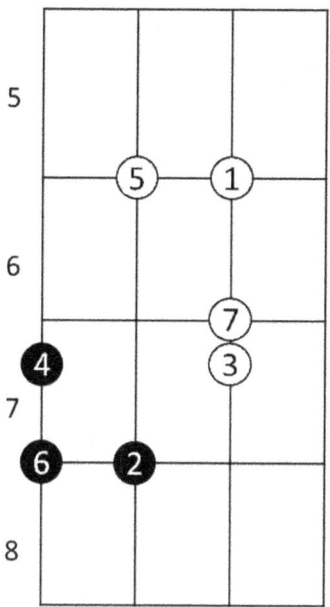

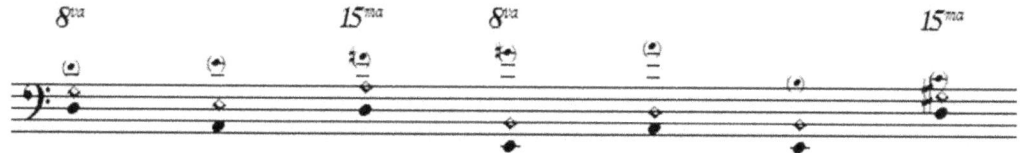

D Dorian

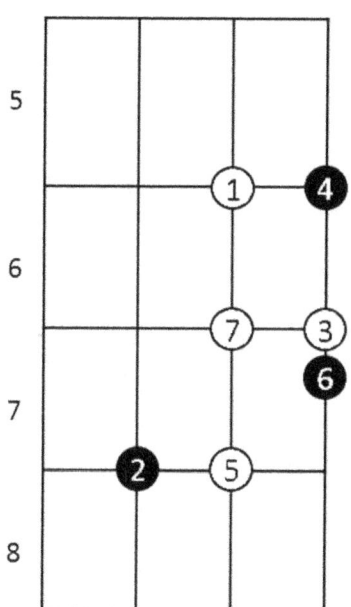

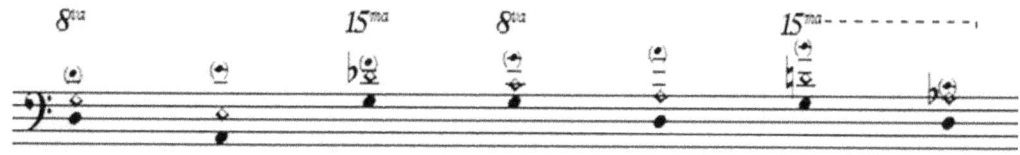

D Mel Minor

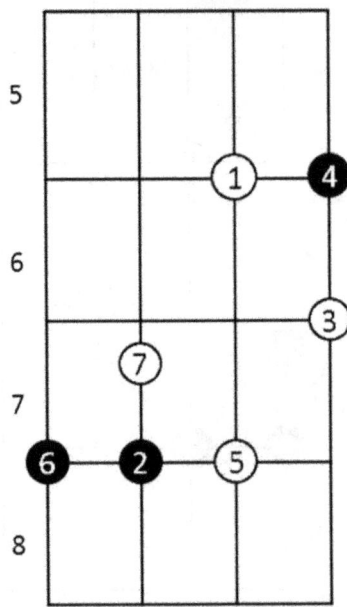

E Mixolydian

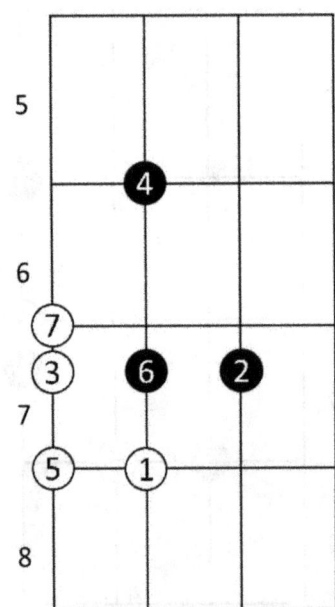

E Mixo b13

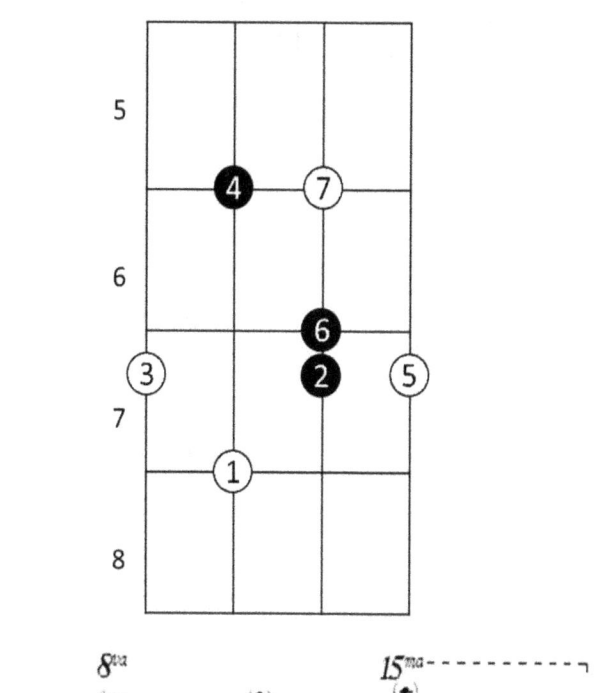

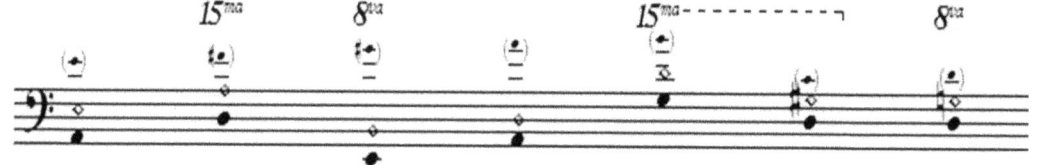

E Mixo b9/b13

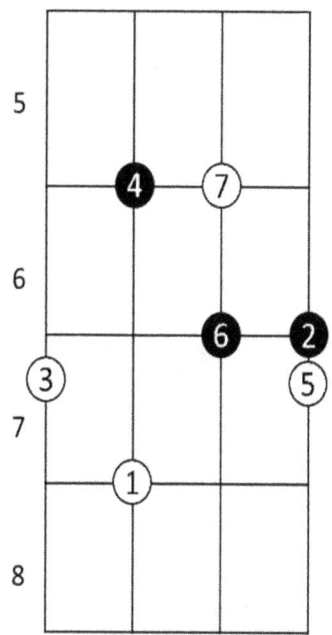

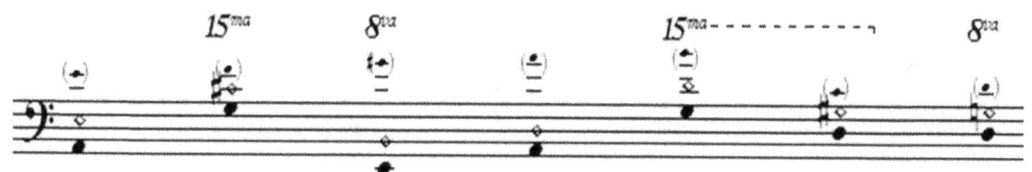

E Aeolian

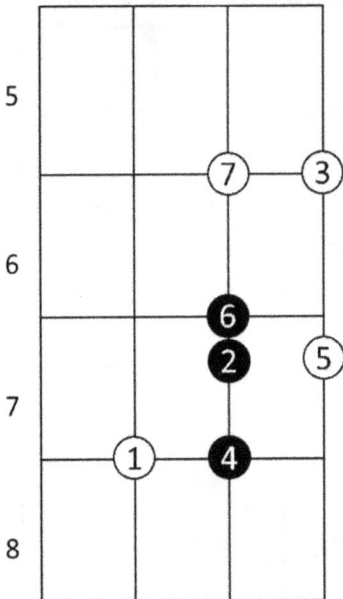

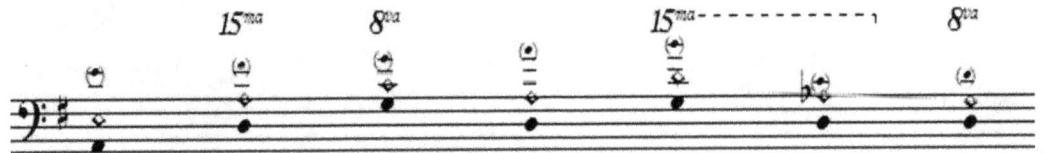

E Dorian

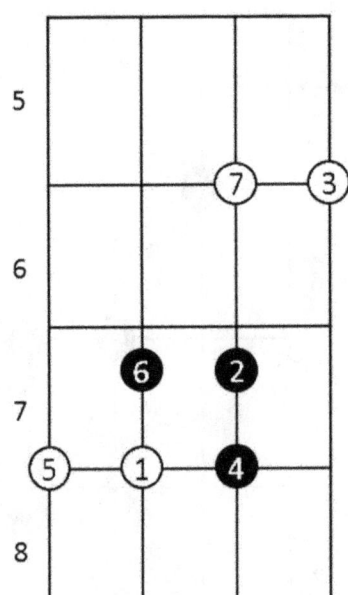

E Altered

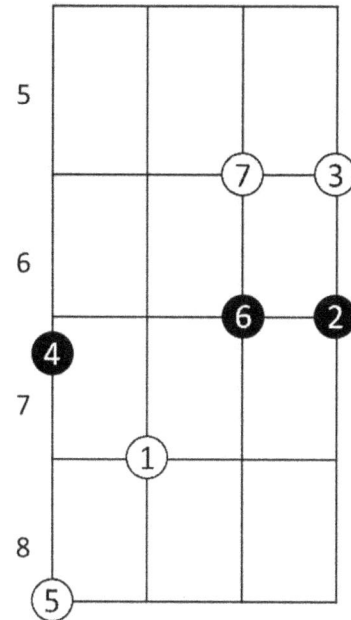

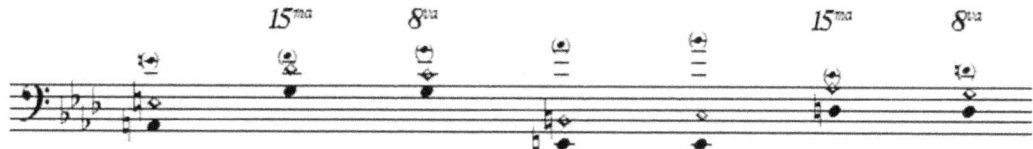

E Phrygian

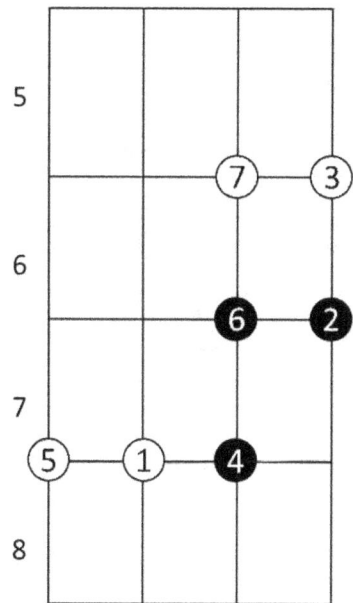

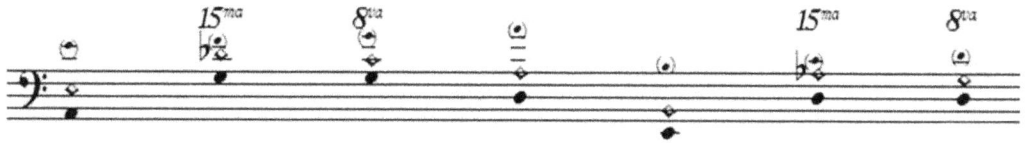

F Lydian

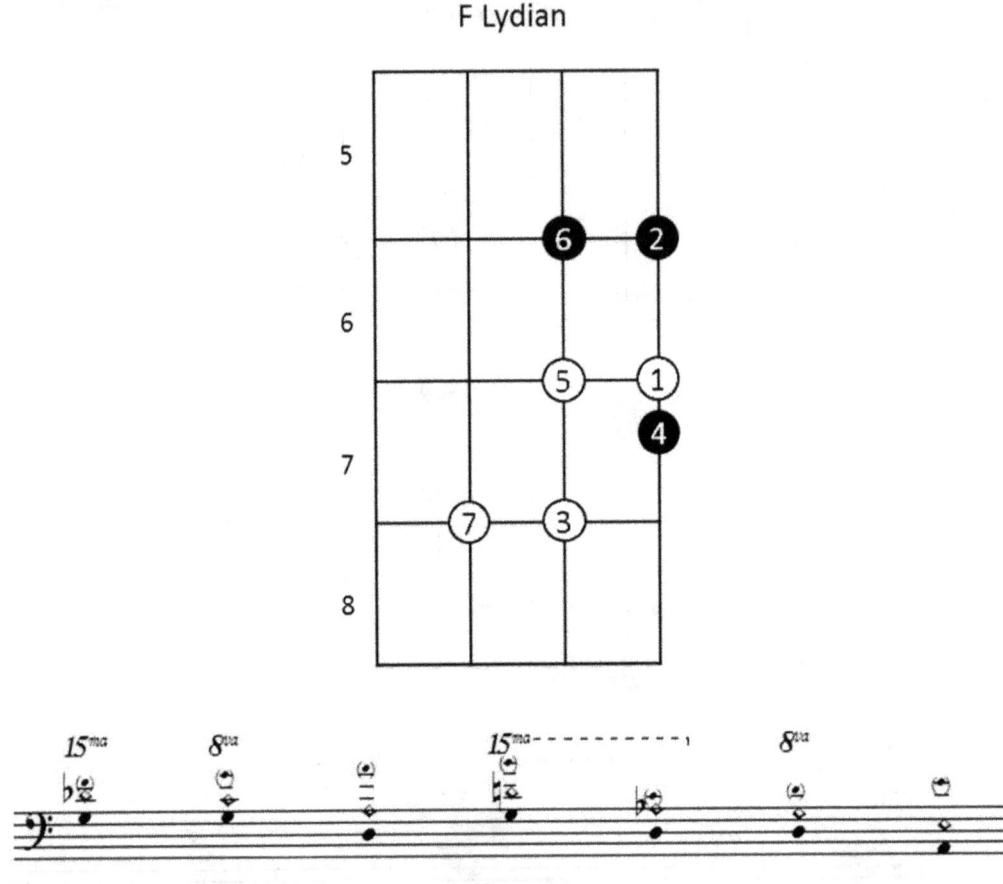

F# Aeolian

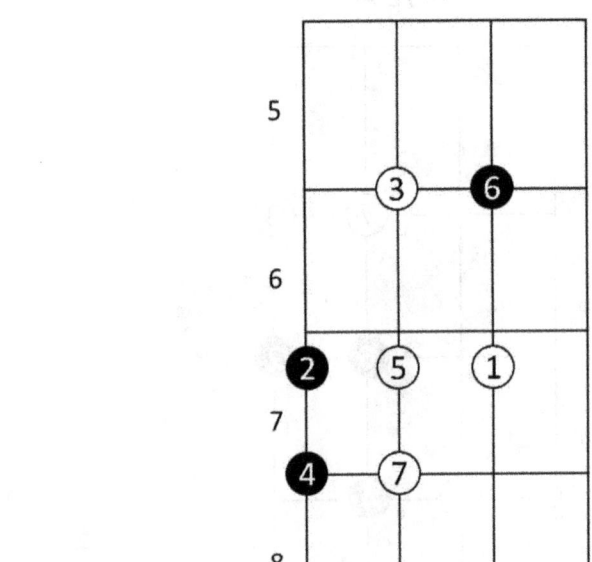

F# Harm Minor

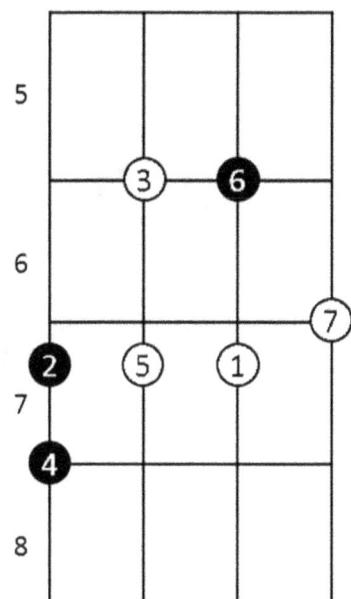

F# Phrygian

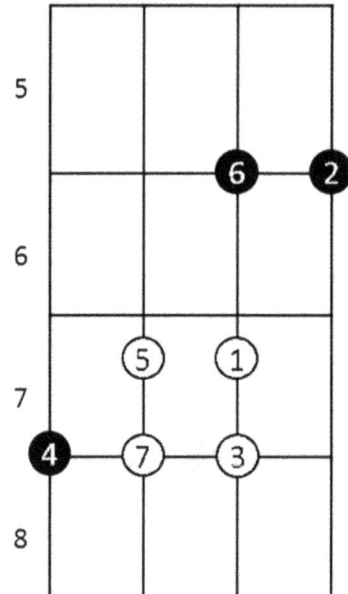

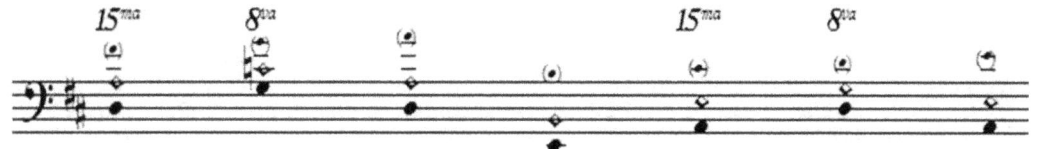

F# Locrian

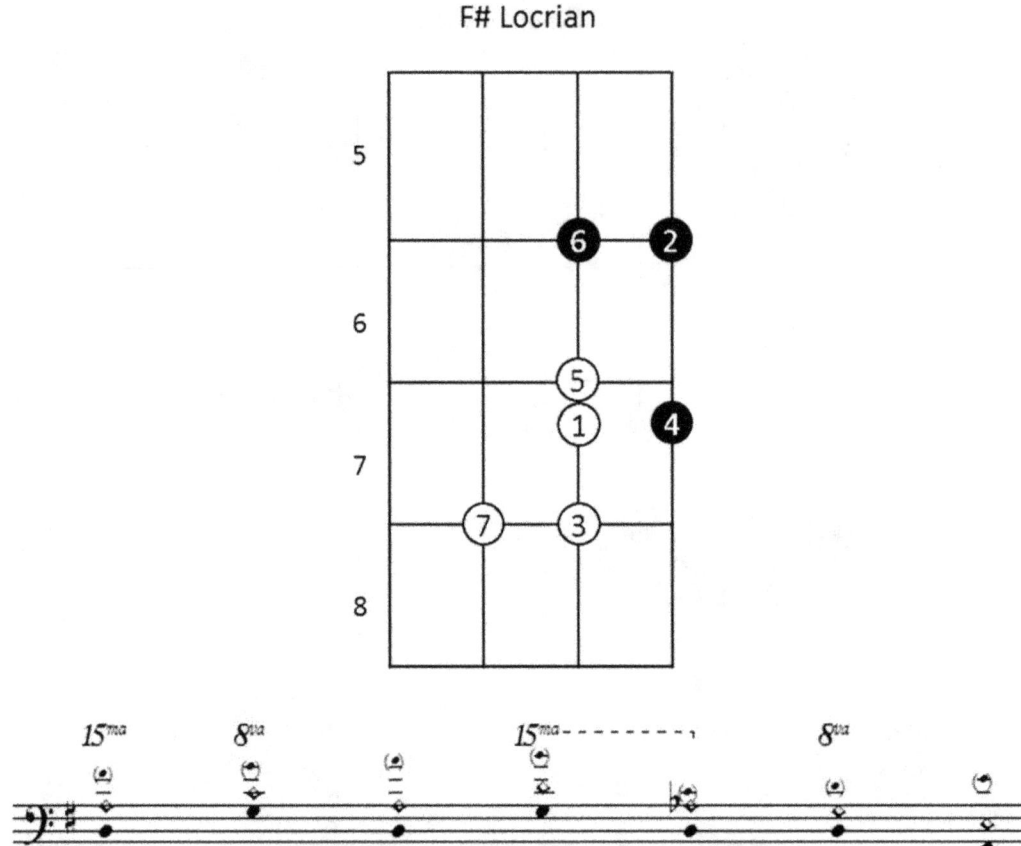

G Ionian

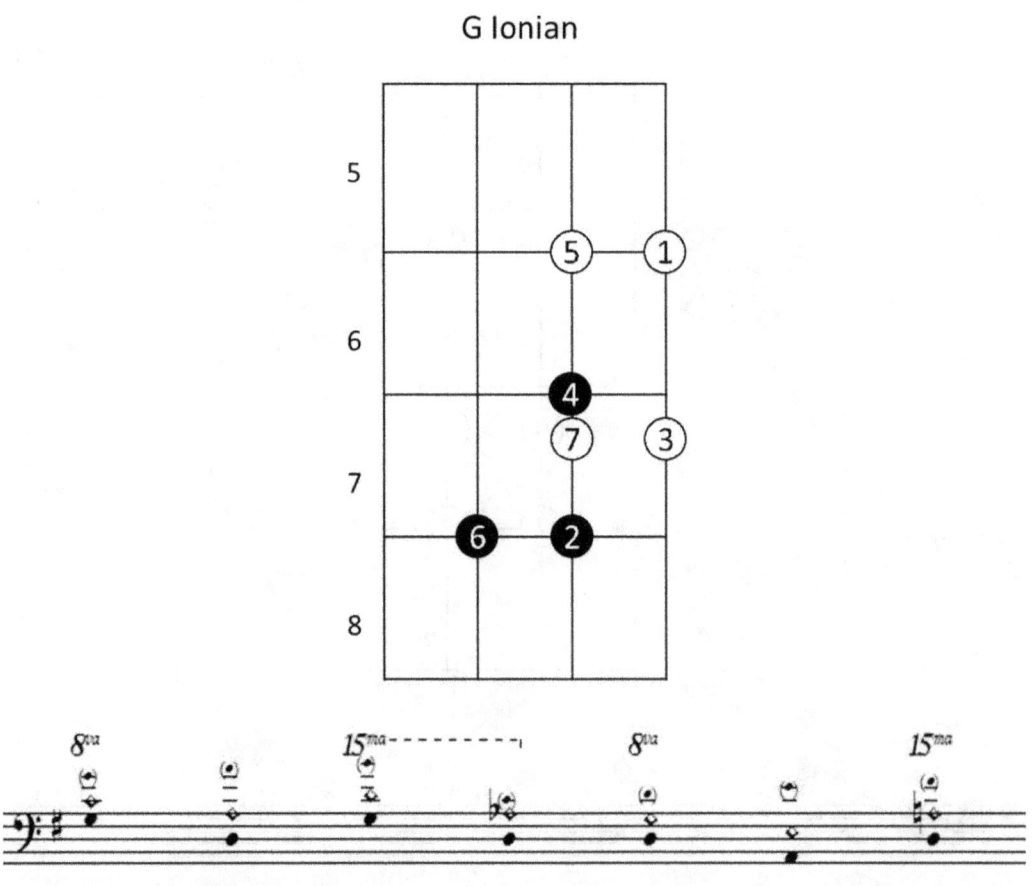

G Lydian

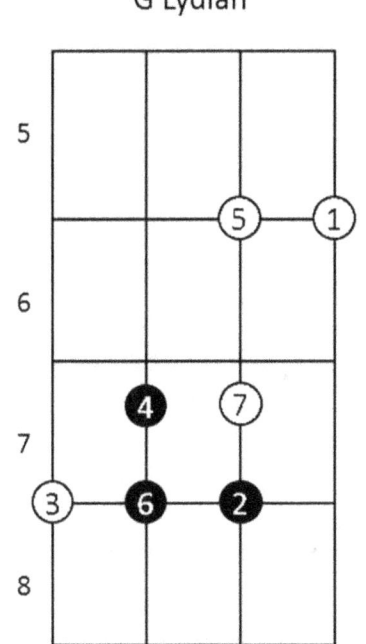

G Mixolydian

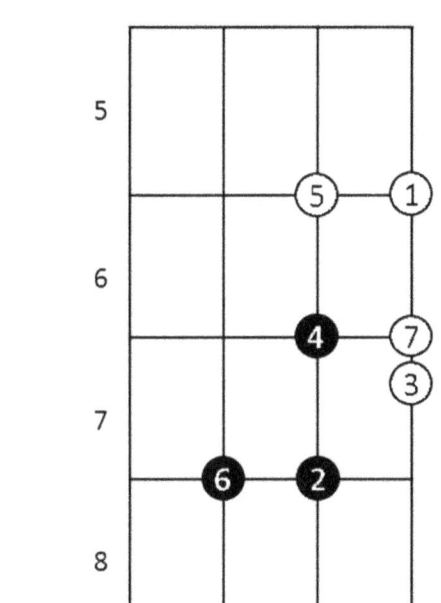

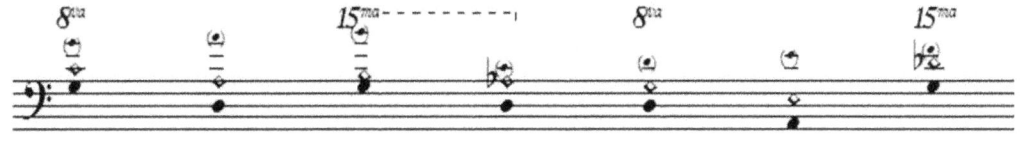

G Mixo #11

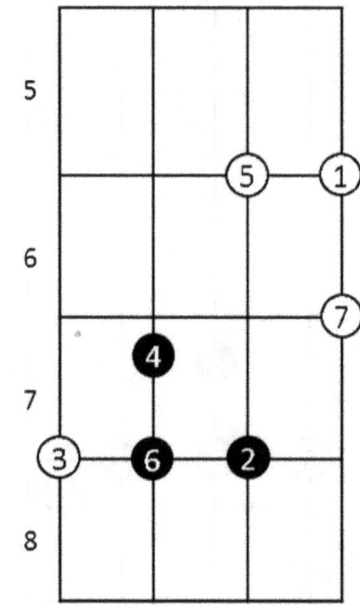

G# Locrian

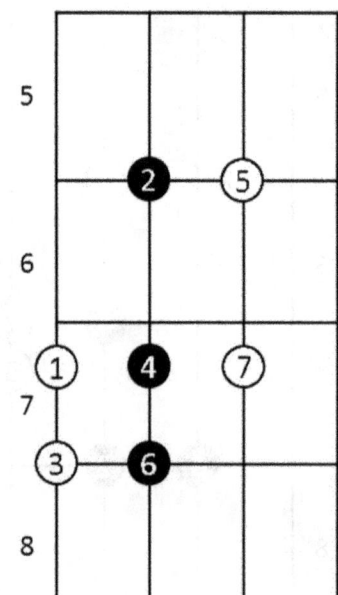

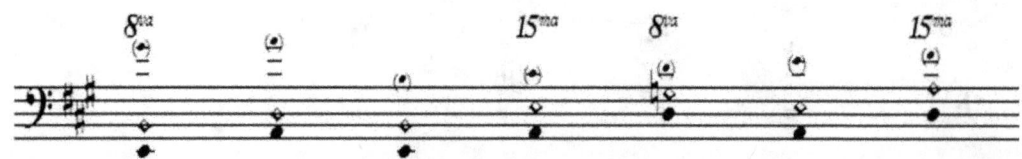

G# Altered

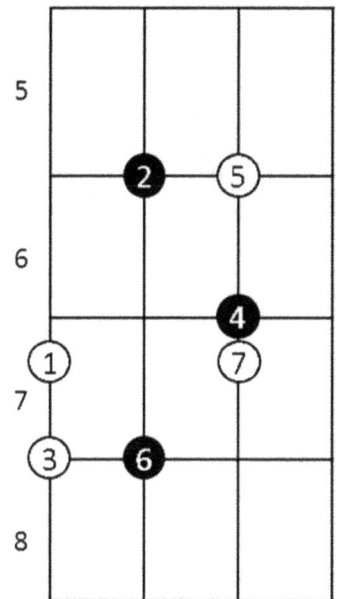

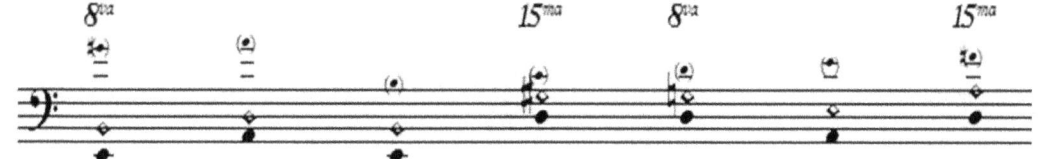

A Ionian

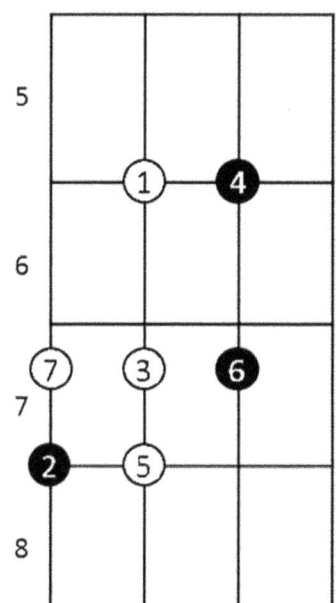

A Mixolydian

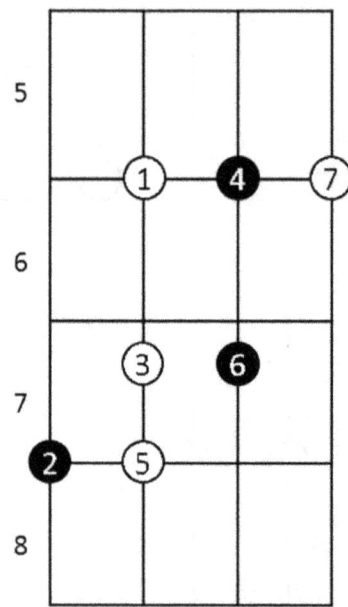

A Mixo b13

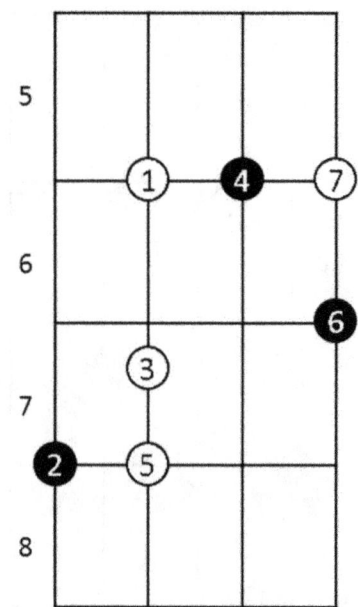

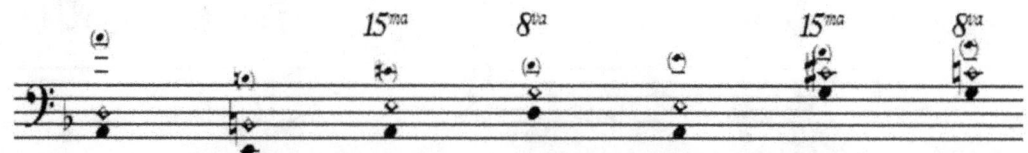

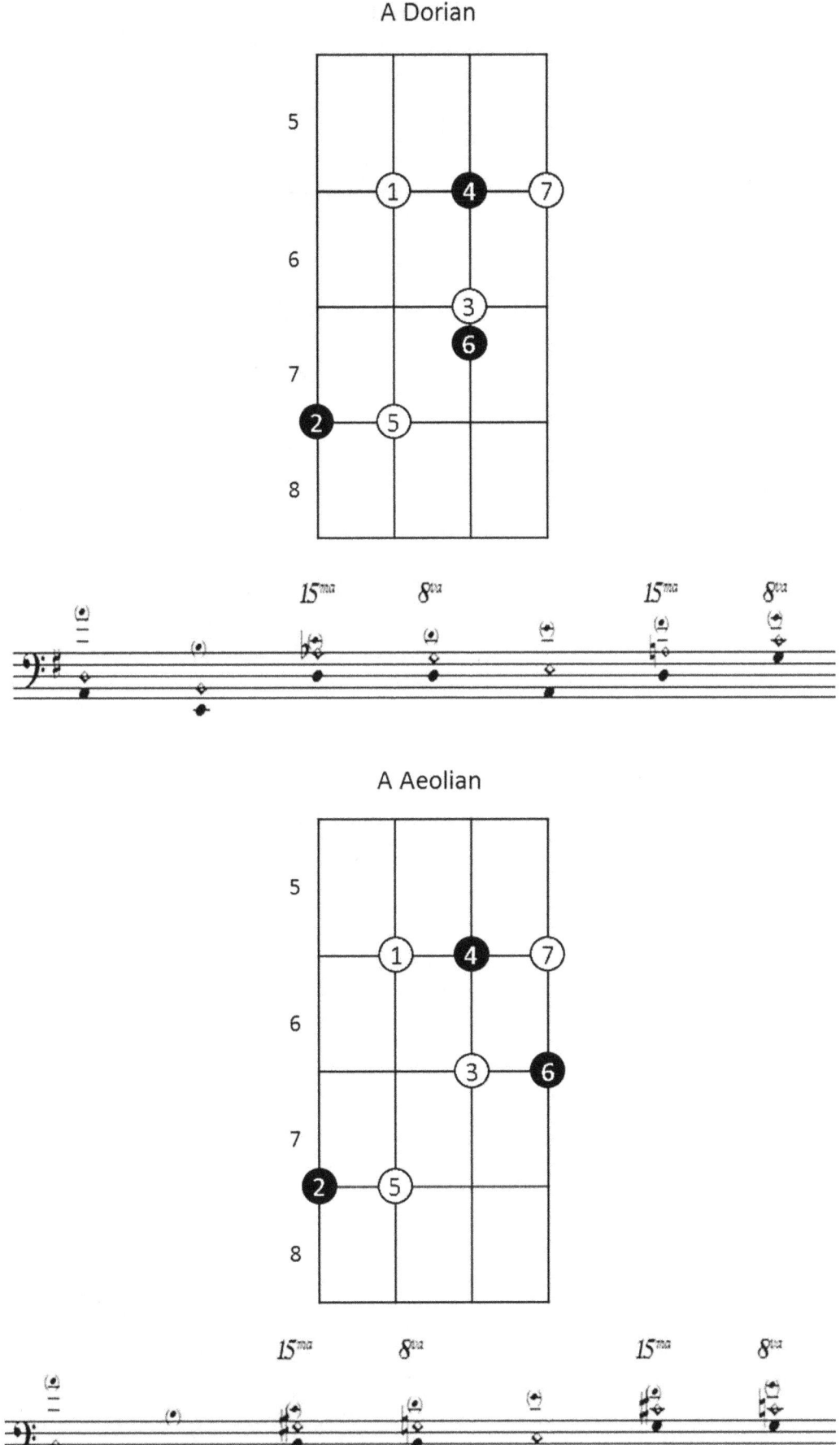

A Harm Minor

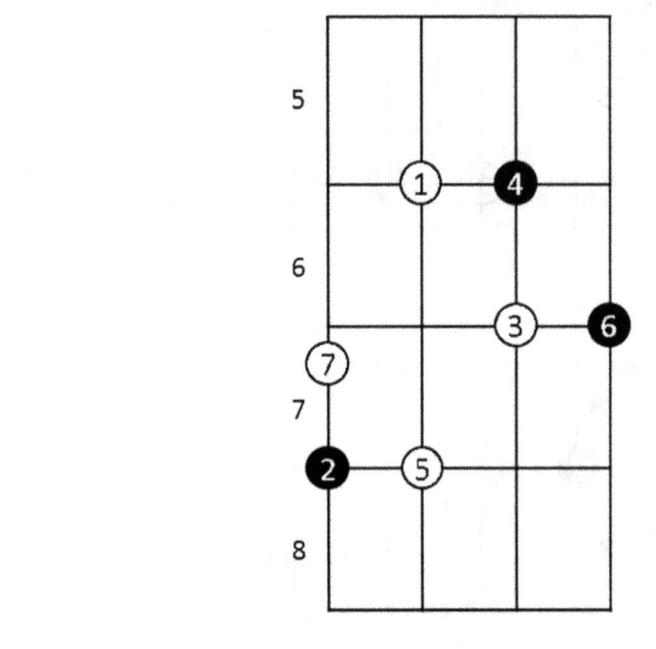

A Mel Minor

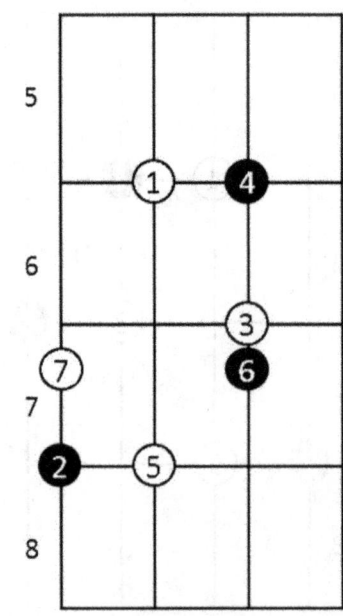

B Locrian

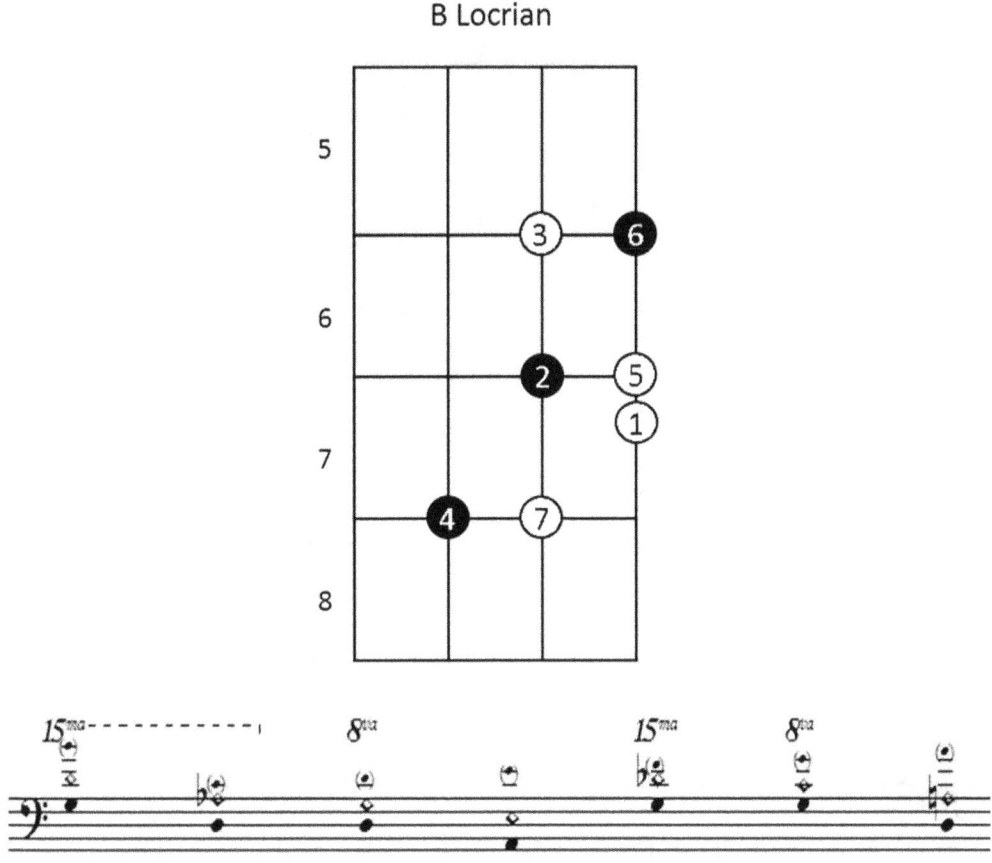

B Phrygian

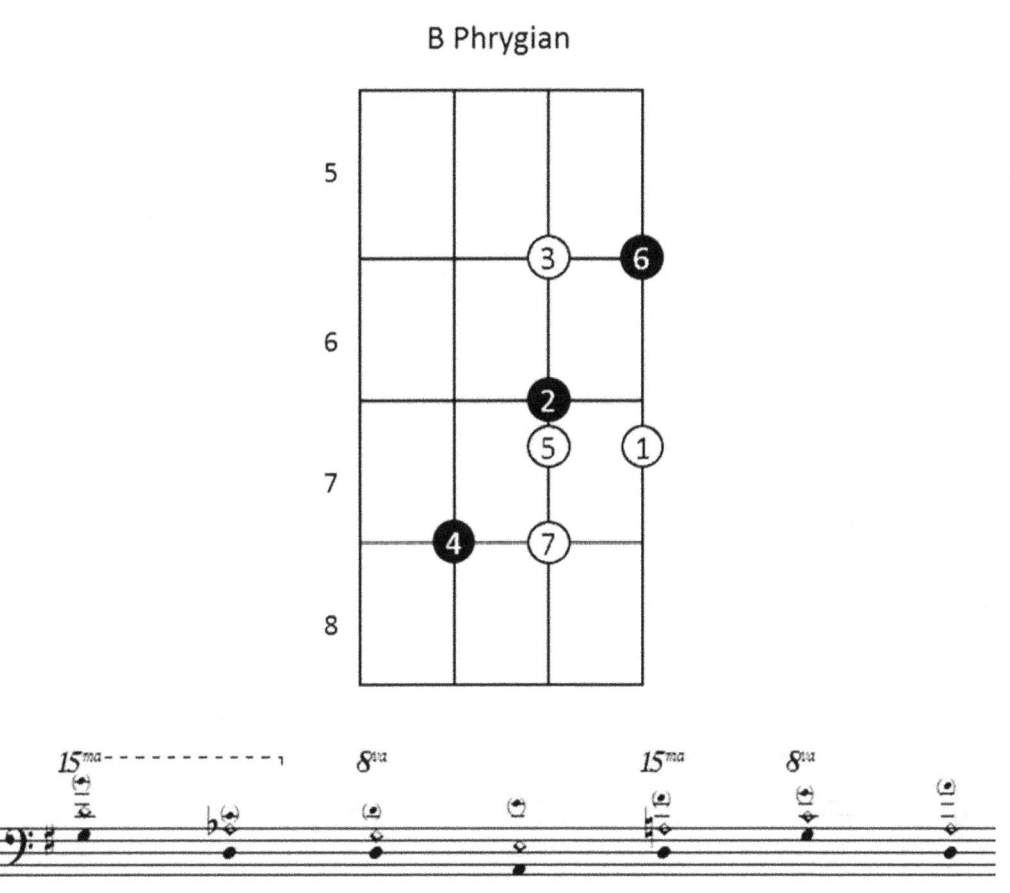

B Dorian

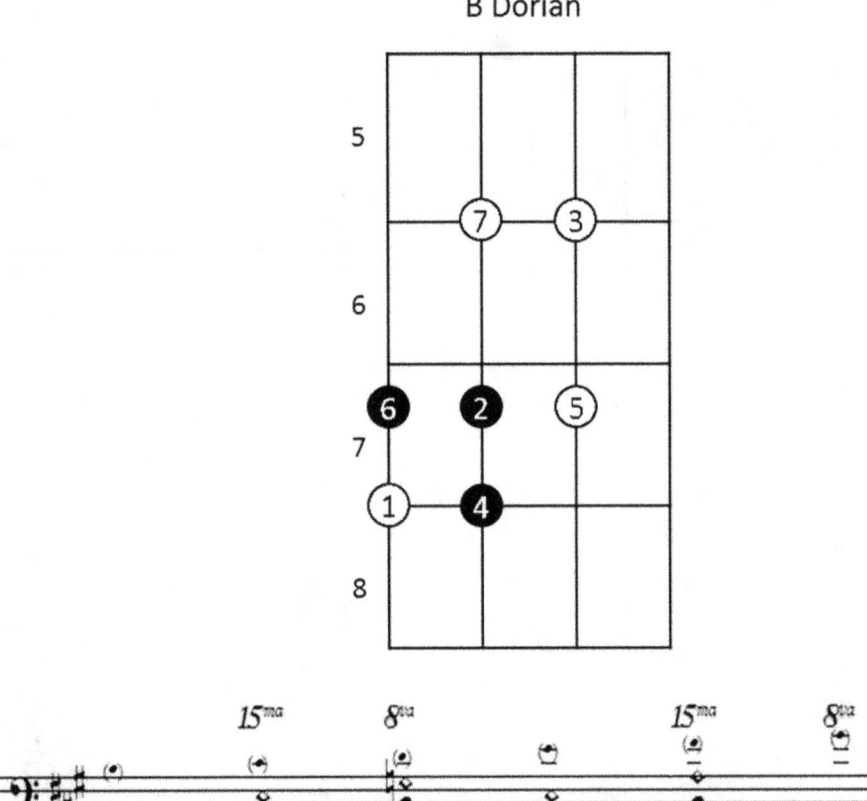

B Aeolian

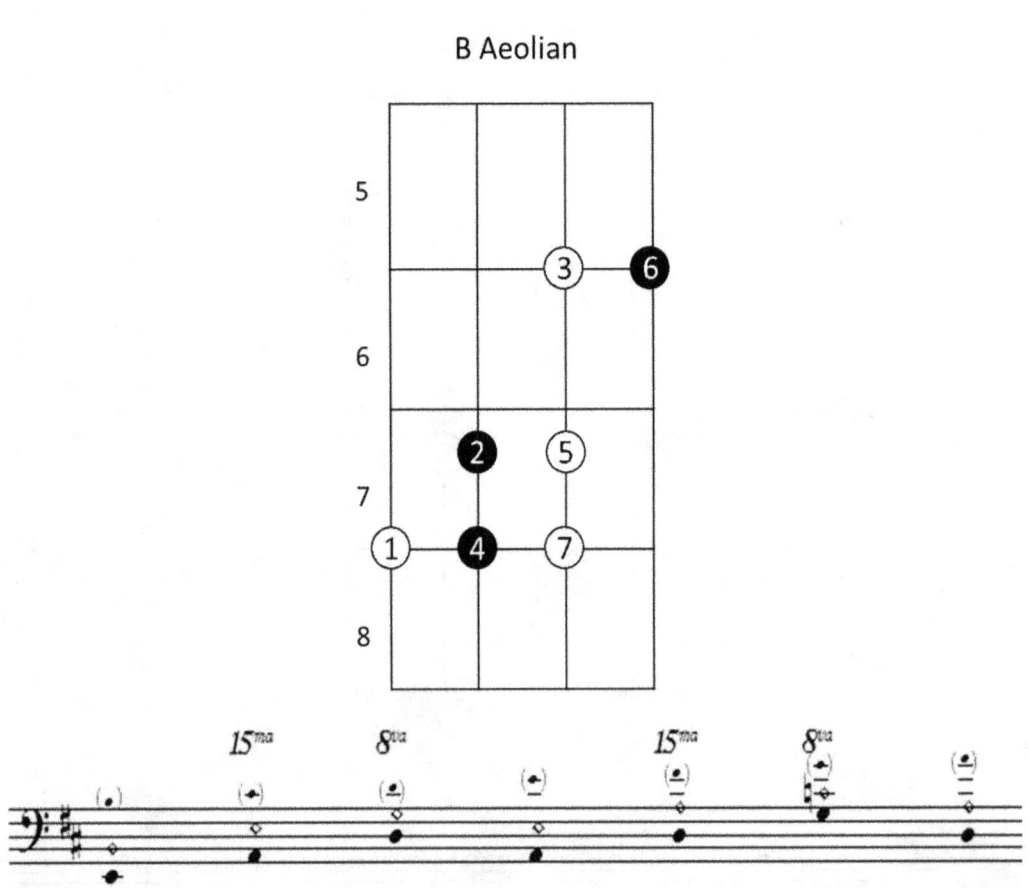

Scales: Chapter 3
3rd Position: Frets 9 - 12

Harmonics between the 9th – 12th frets

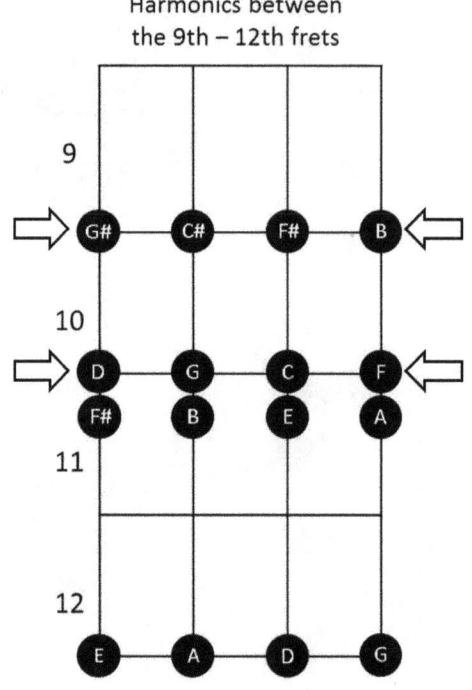

C Ionian

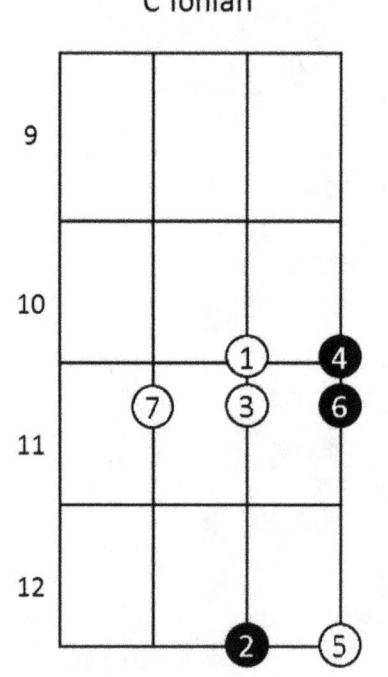

C Lydian

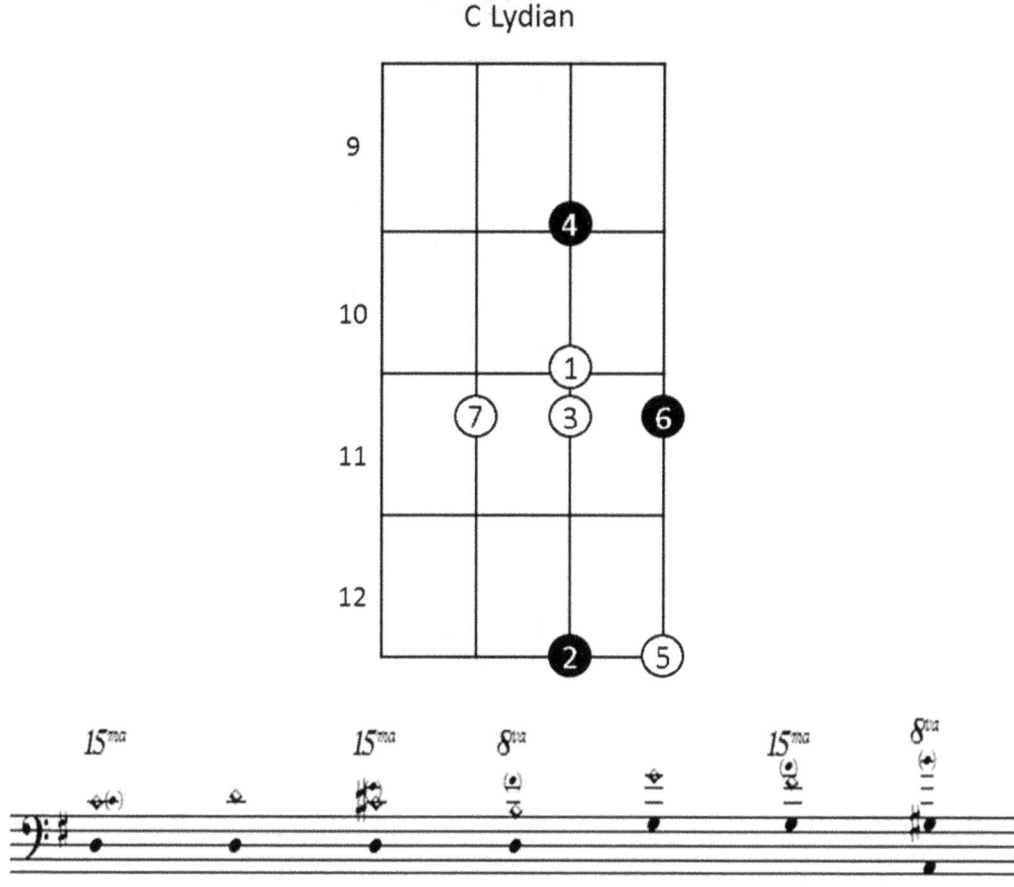

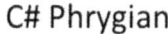

C# Phrygian

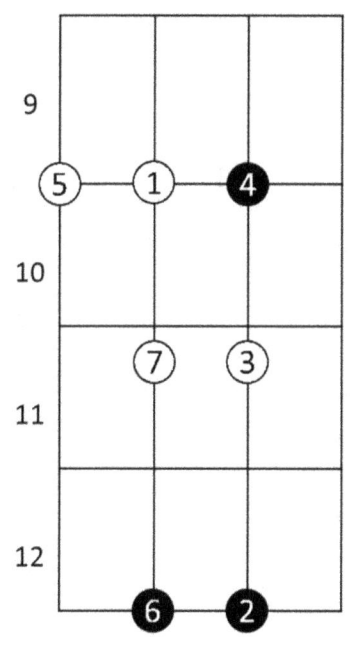

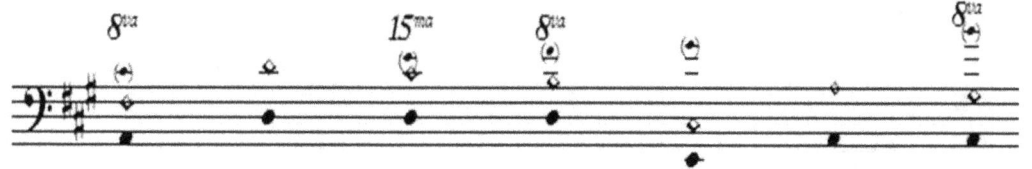

C# Locrian

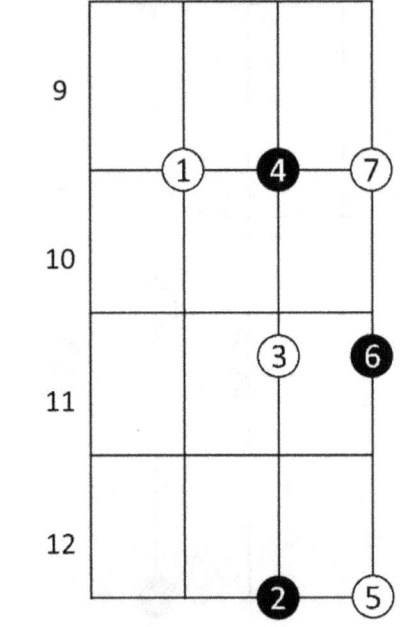

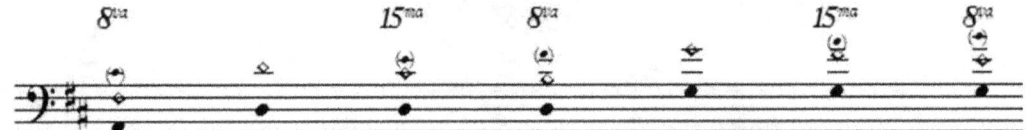

C# Altered

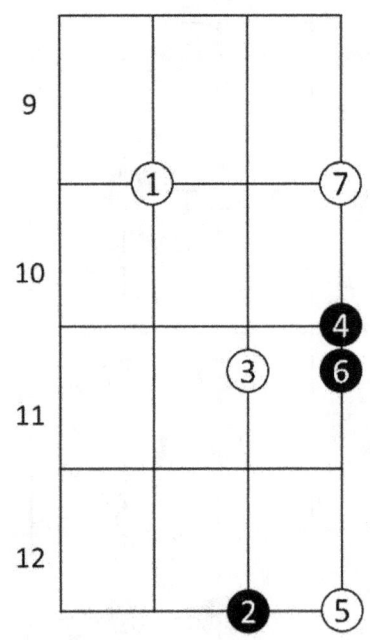

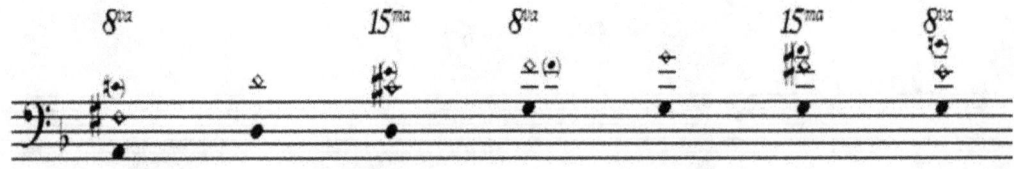

C# Mixo b9/b13

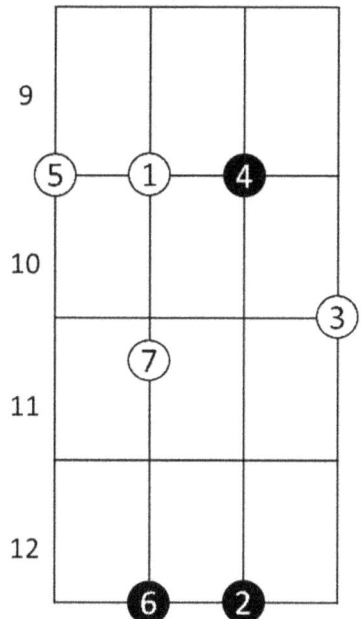

D Ionian

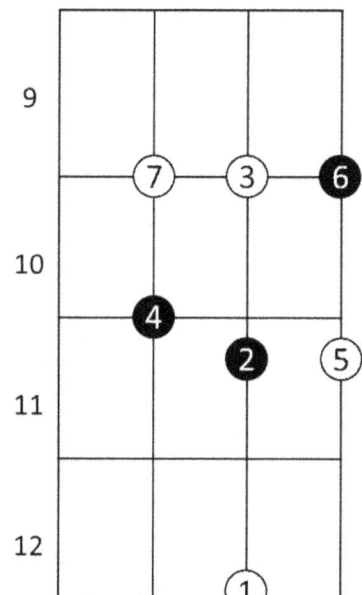

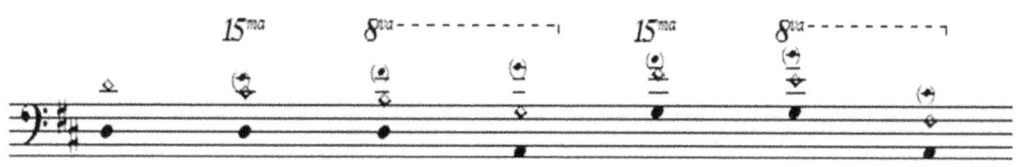

D Mixolydian

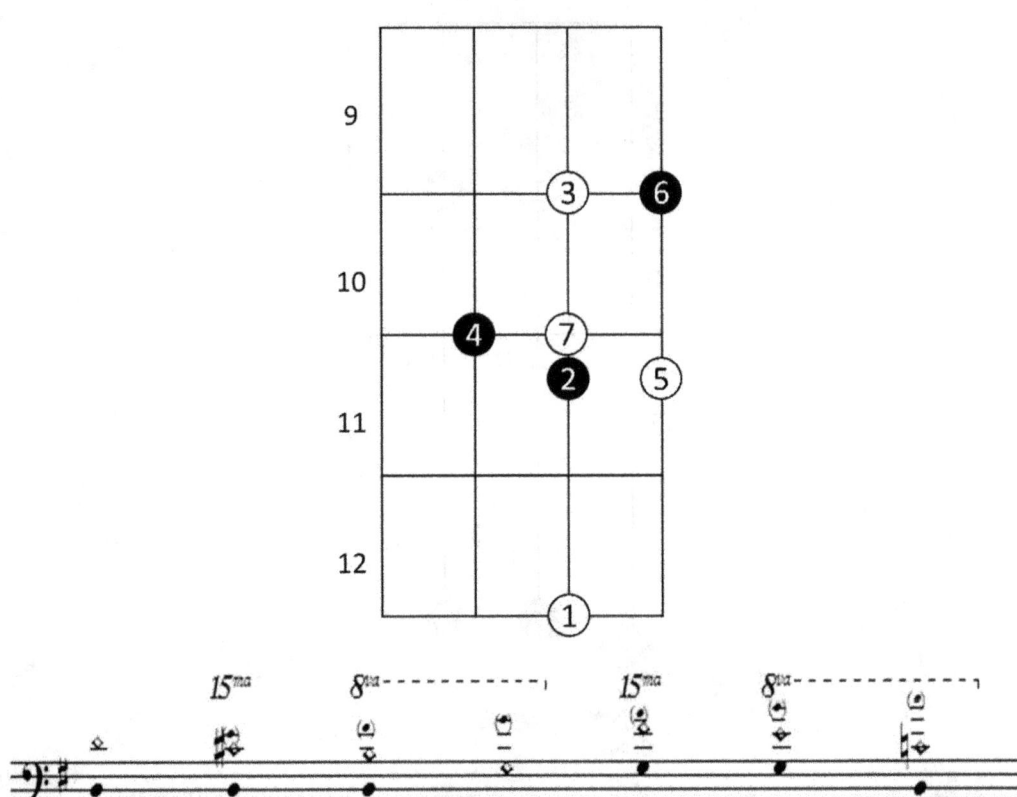

D Lydian

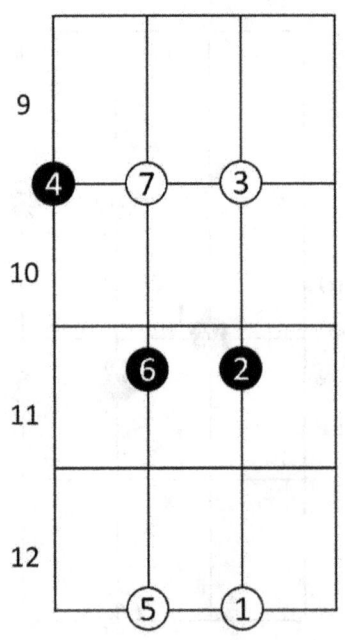

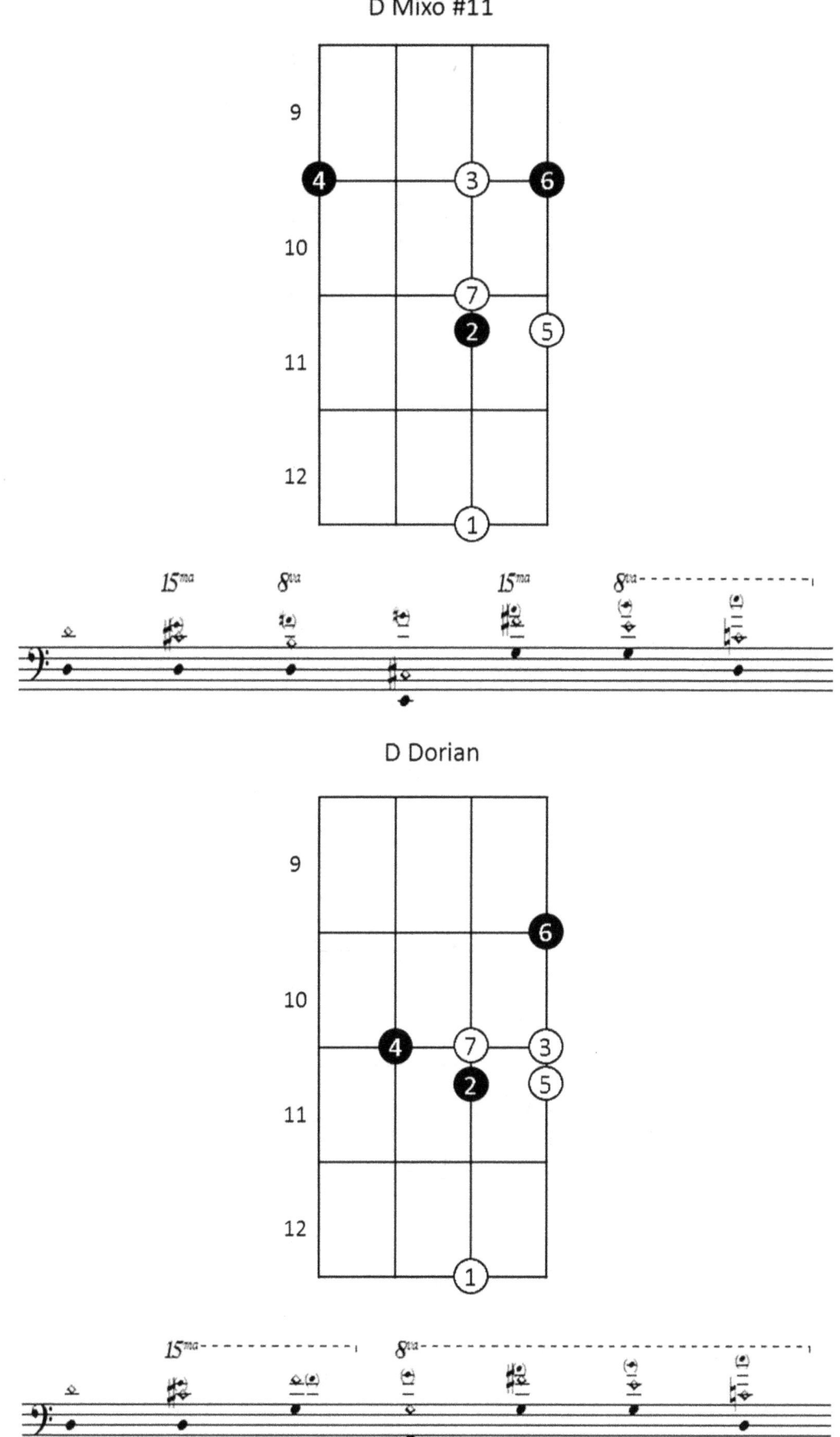

D Mel Minor

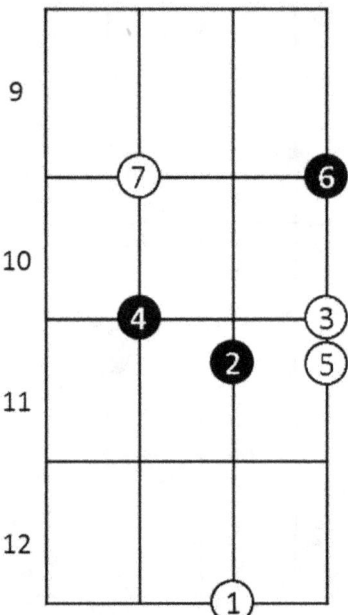

E Mixolydian

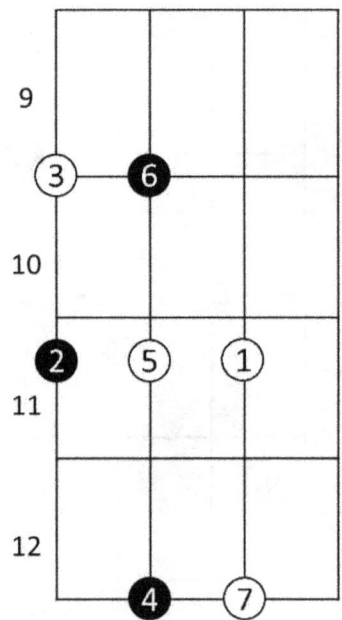

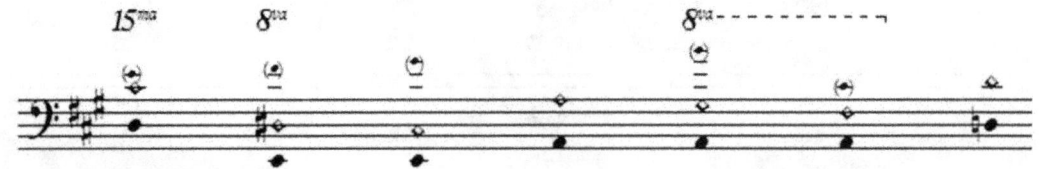

E Mixo b13

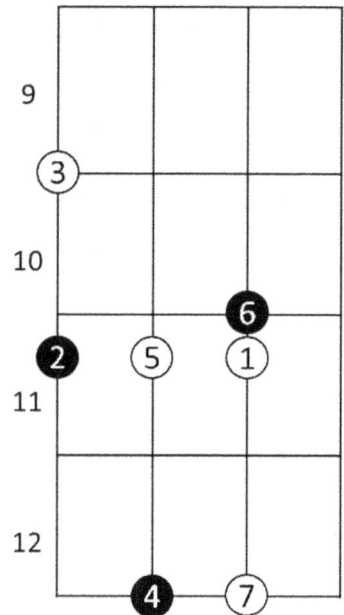

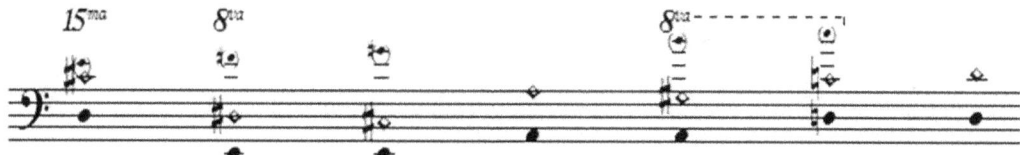

E Mixo b9/b13

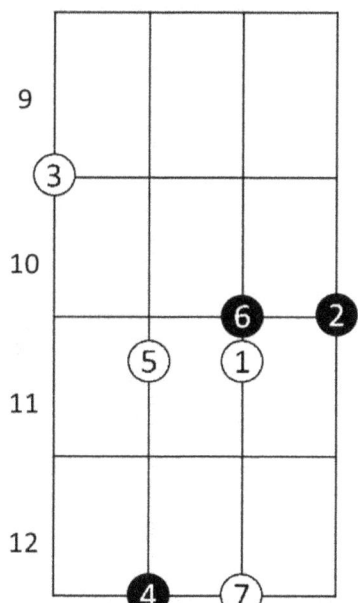

E Aeolian

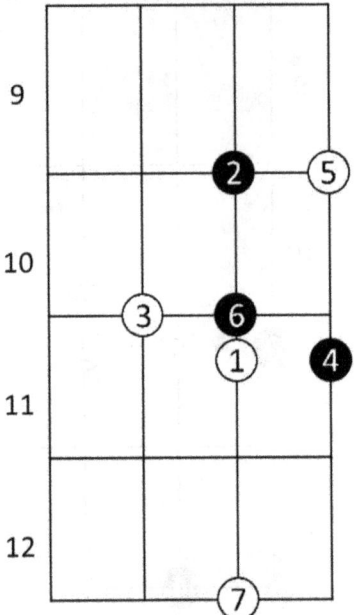

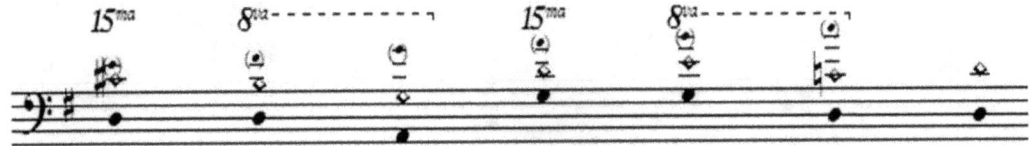

E Phrygian

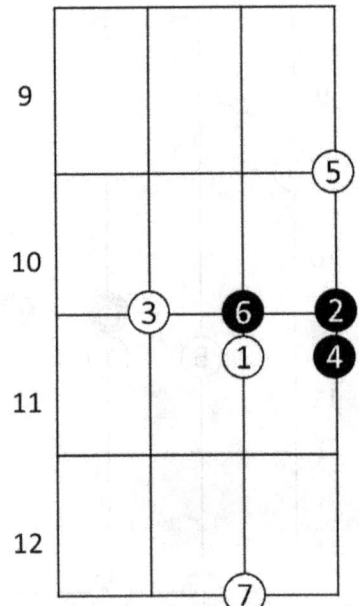

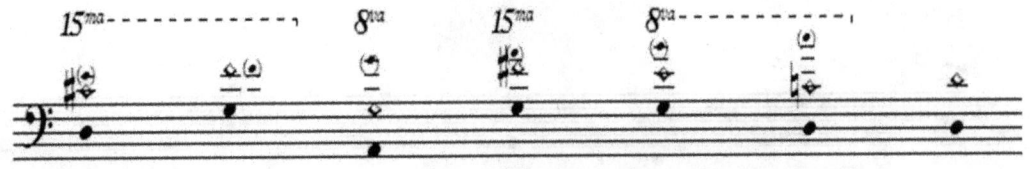

E Dorian

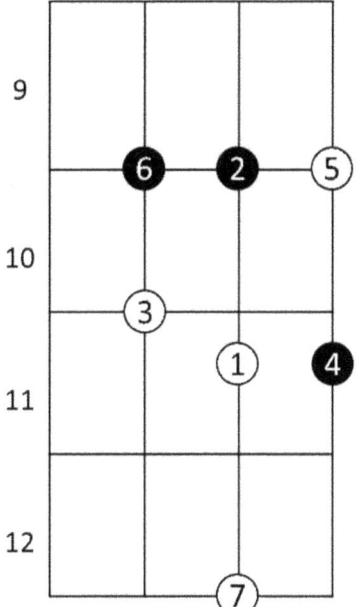

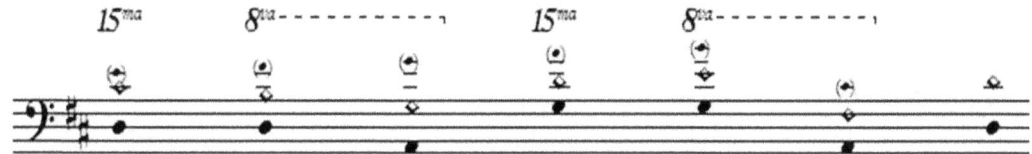

F Lydian

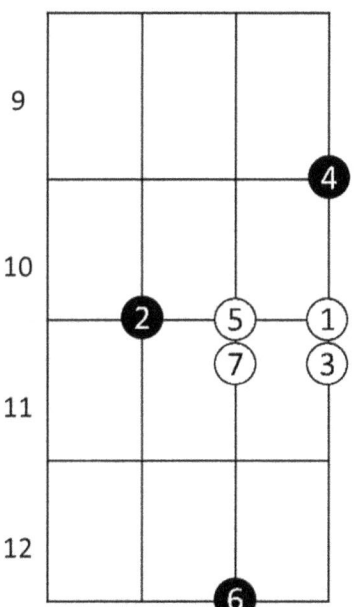

F# Locrian

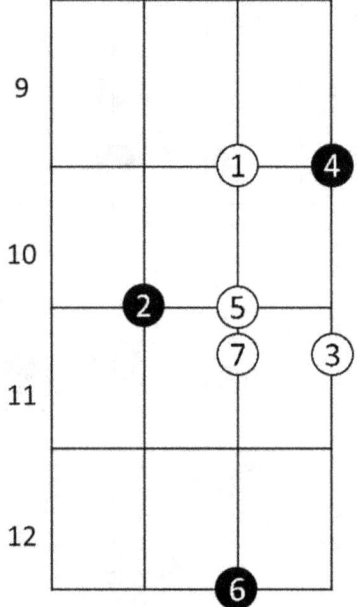

F# Phrygian

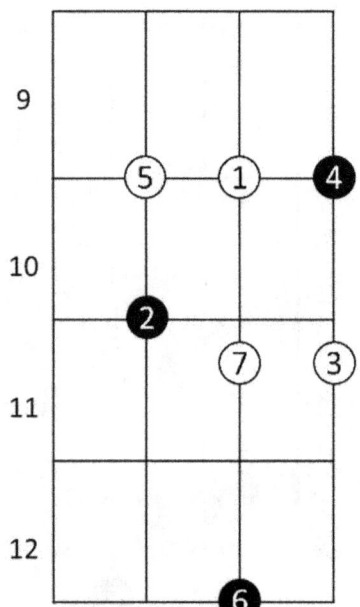

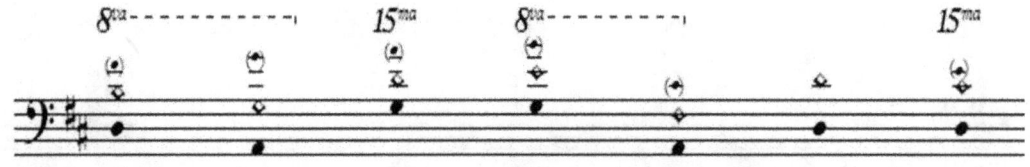

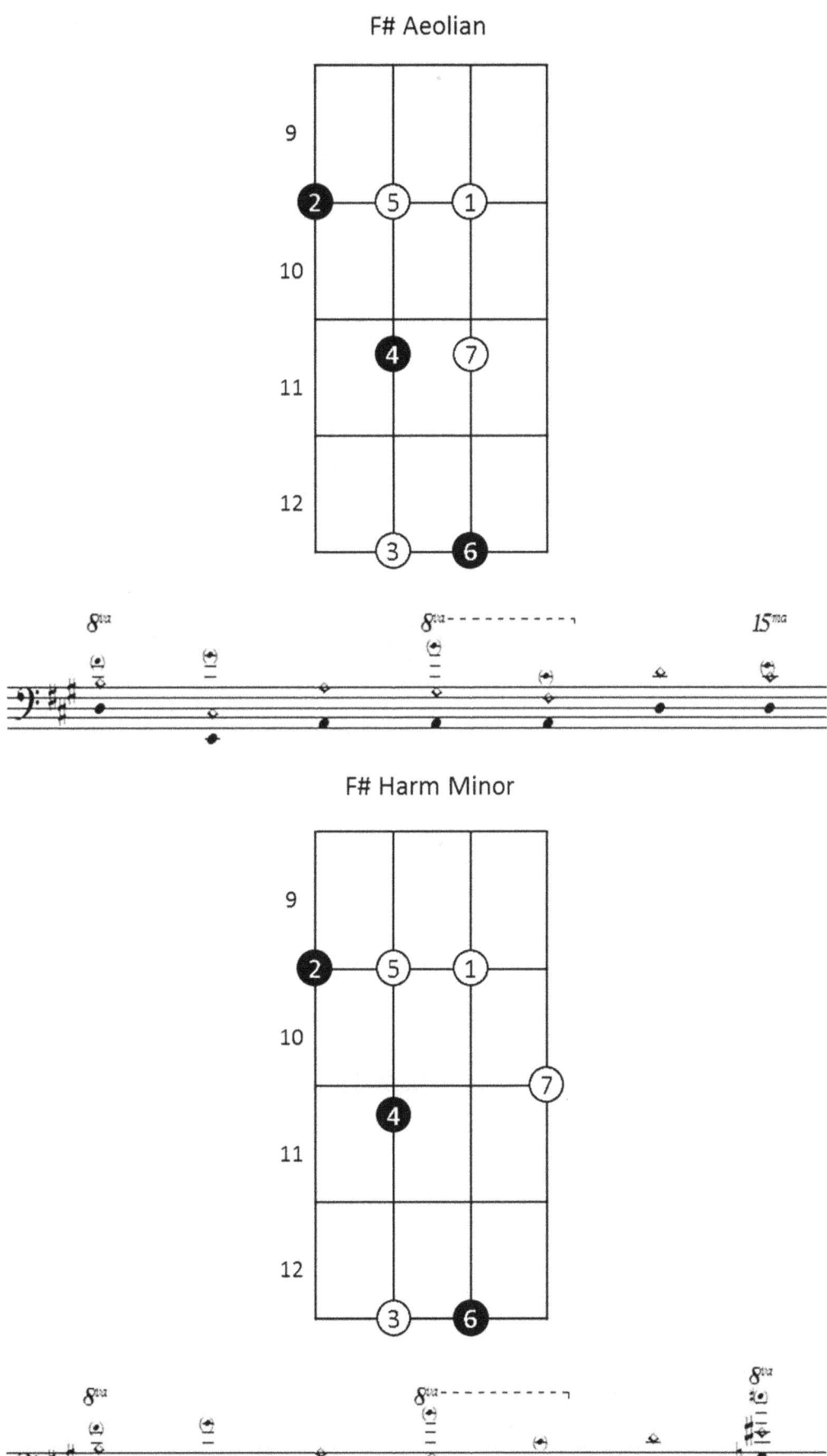

G Ionian

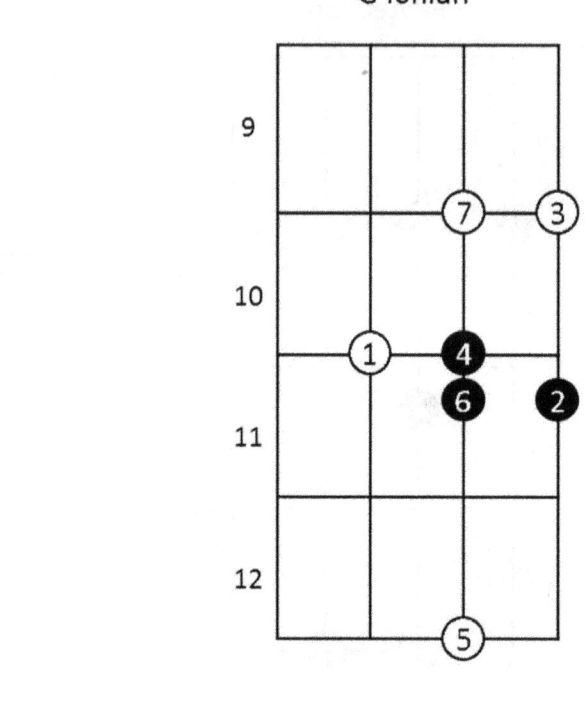

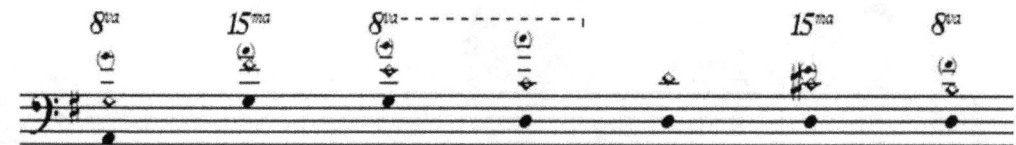

G Lydian

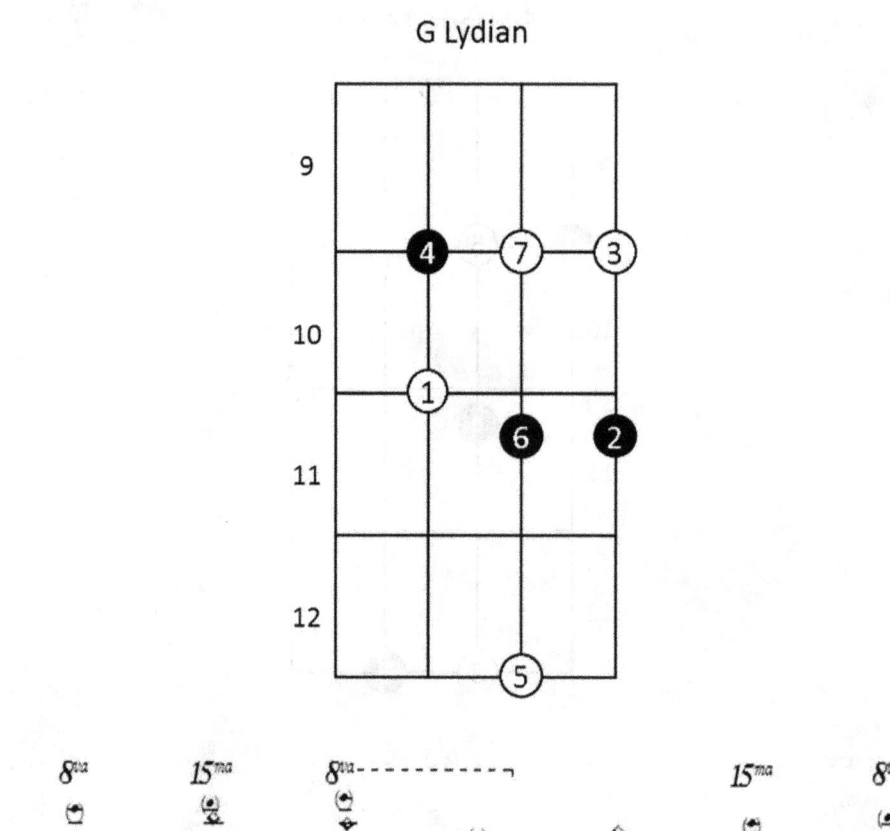

G Mixolydian

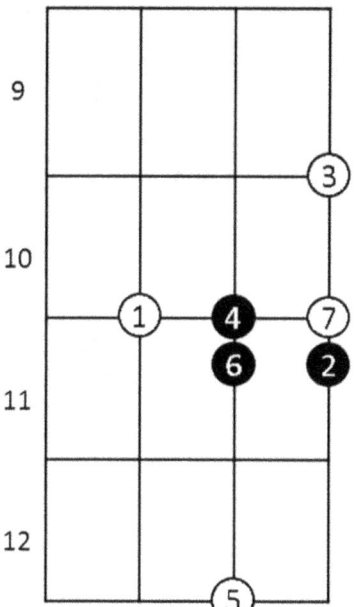

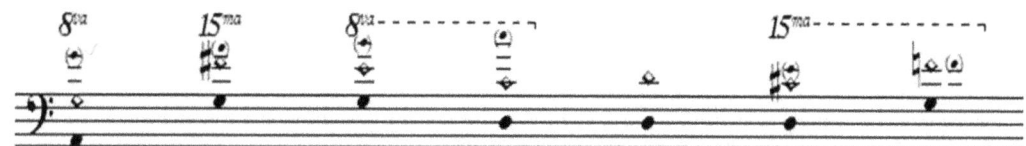

G Mixo #11

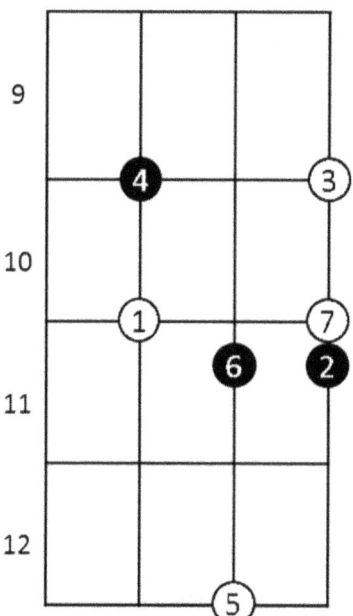

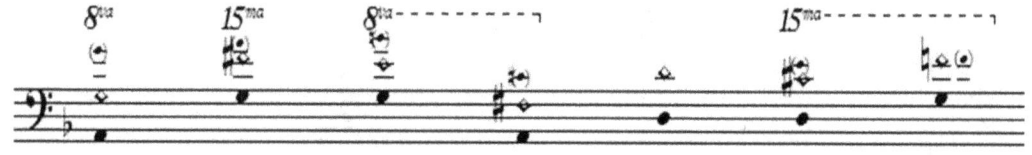

G# Locrian

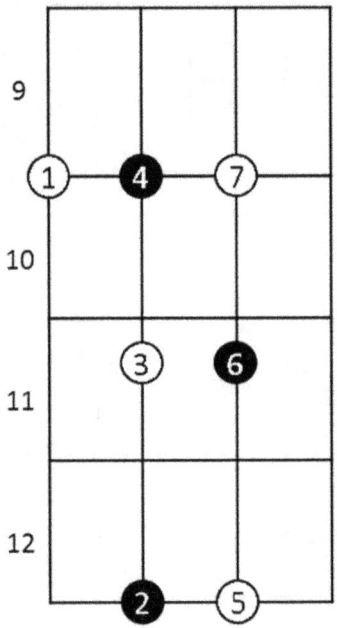

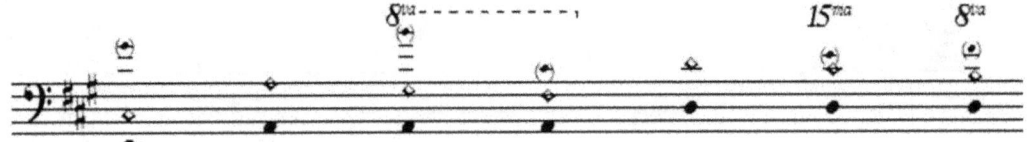

G# Altered

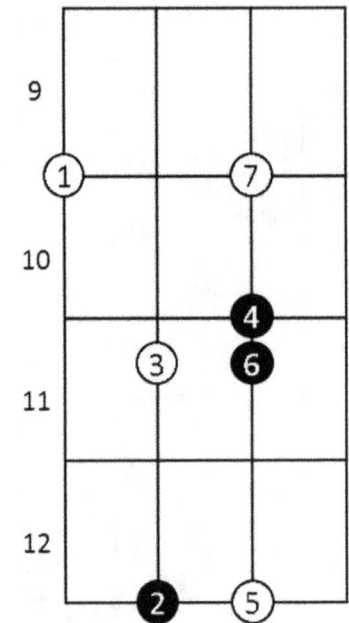

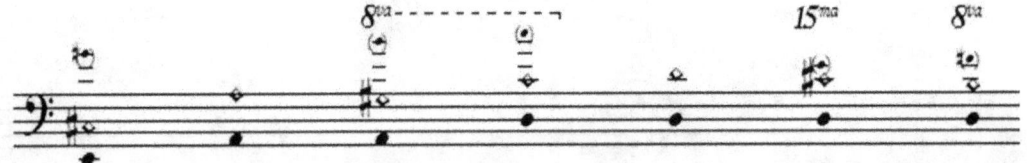

A Ionian

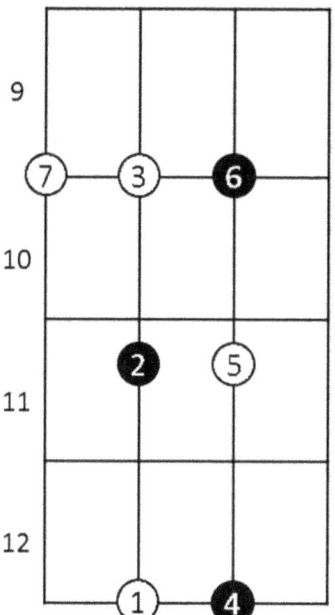

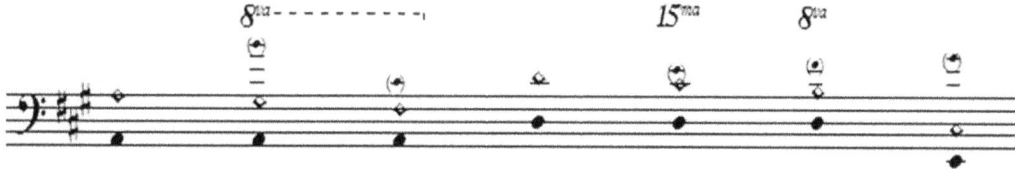

A Mixolydian

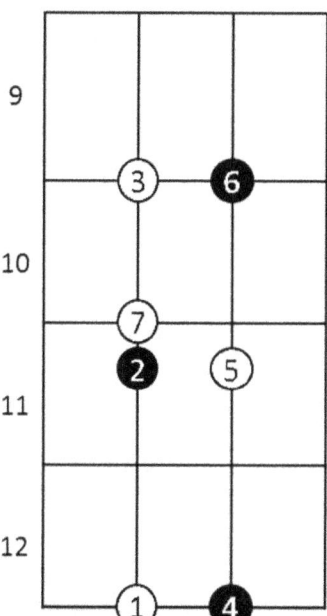

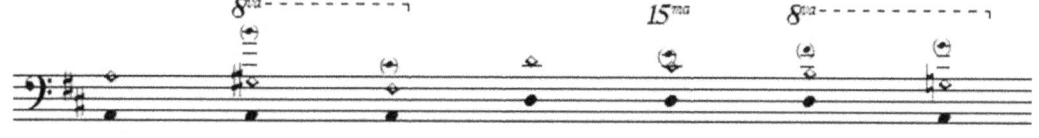

A Aeolian

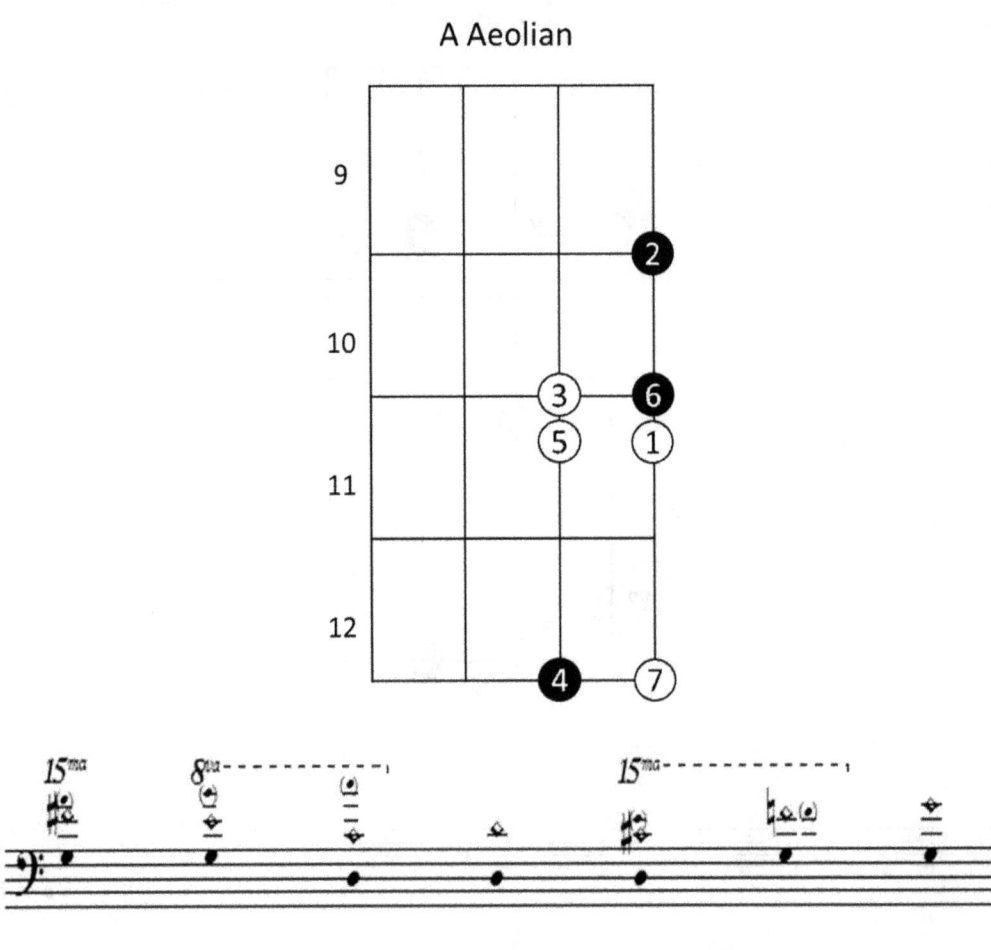

A Dorian

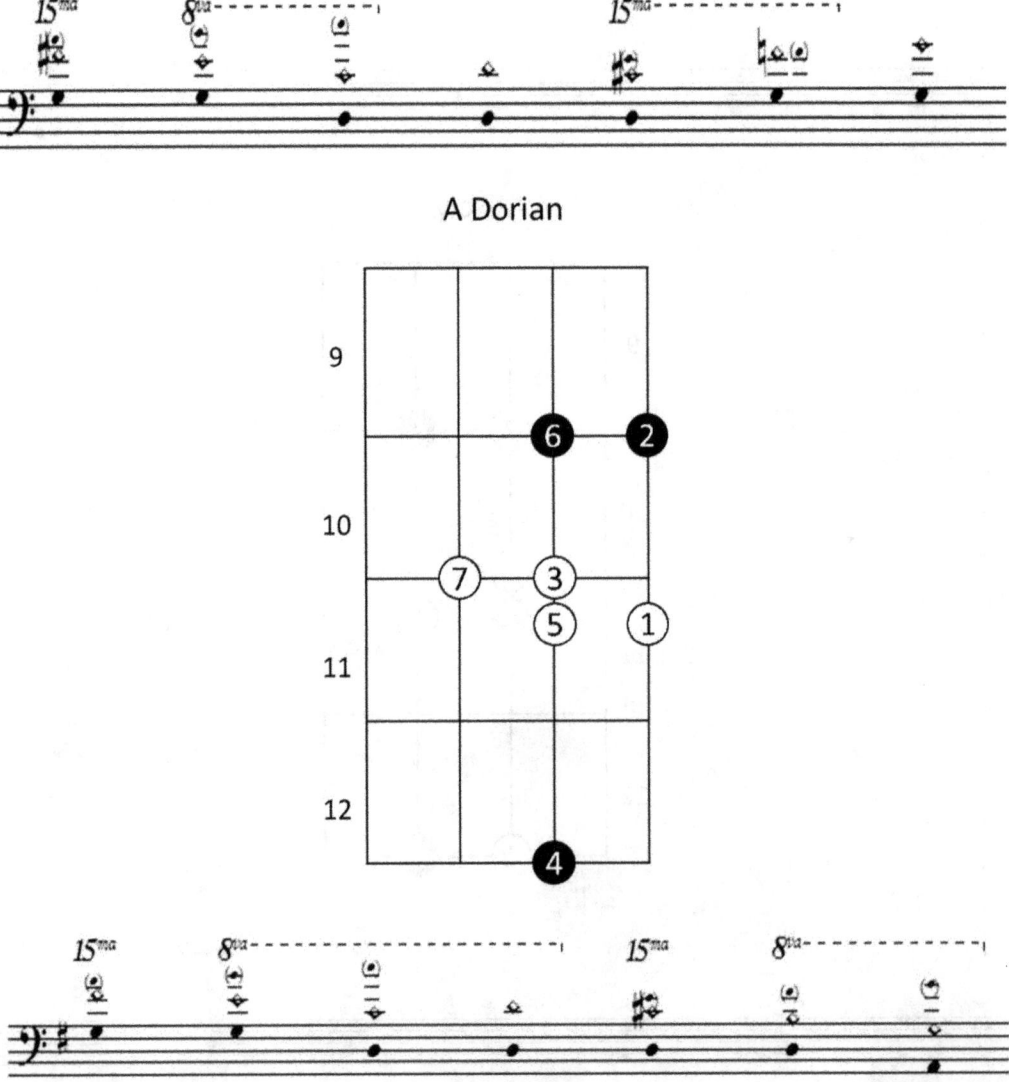

A Harm Minor

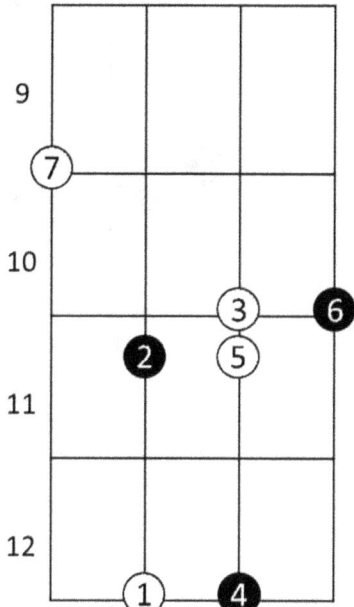

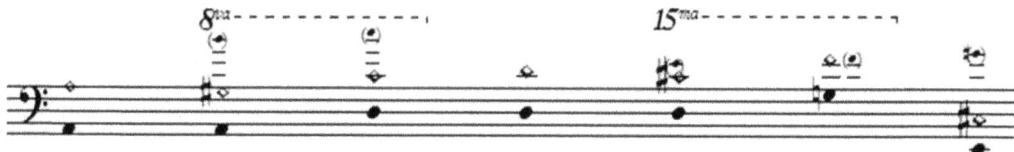

A Mel Minor

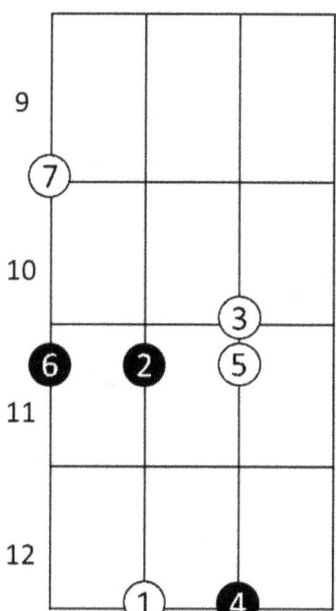

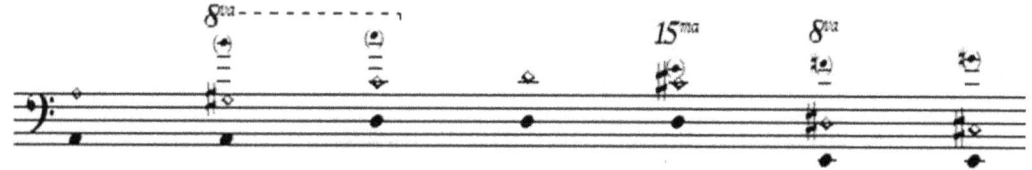

B Aeolian

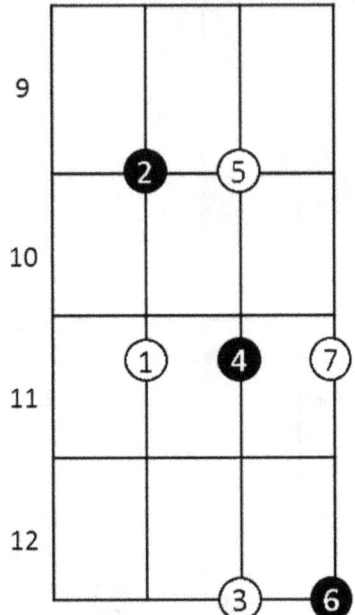

B Dorian

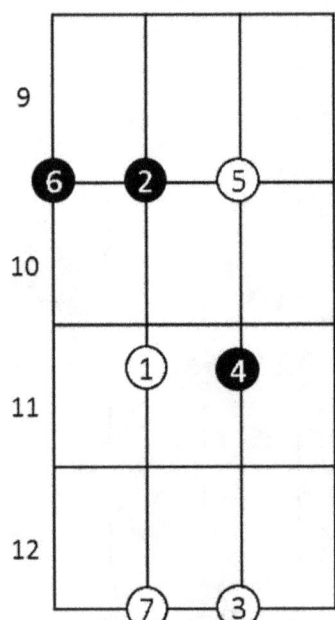

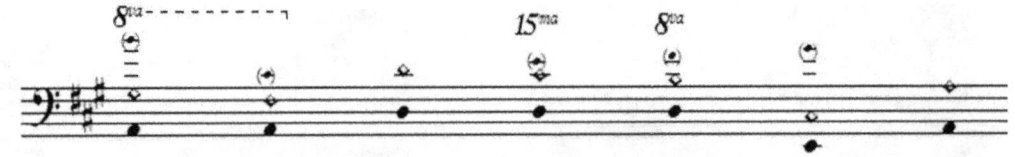

B Phrygian

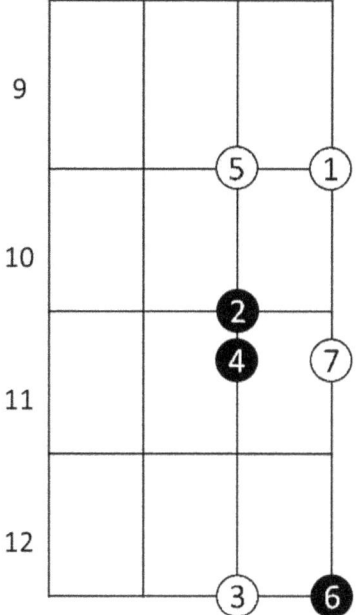
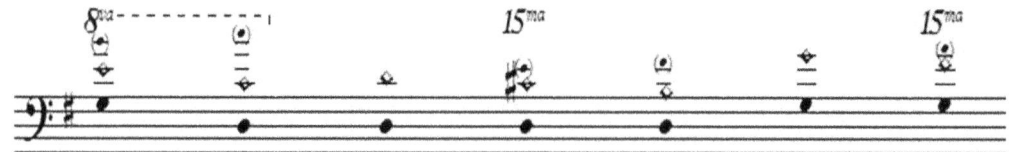

B Locrian

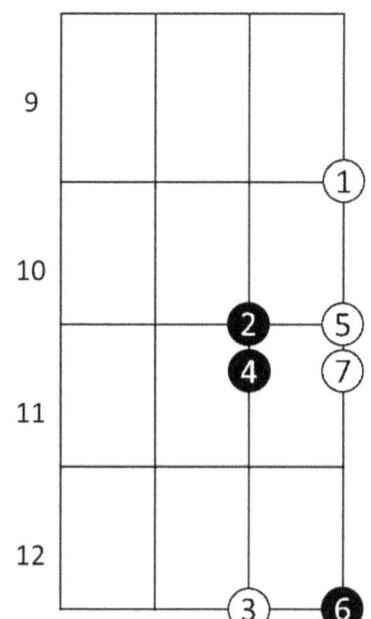

Chords: Chapter 1
1ˢᵗ Position : Frets 2 - 5

Your first instinct may be to construct chords using the list of available harmonics. Unlike scales and arpeggios, however, extra care must be taken when building chords. I completely avoided mixing out-of-tune harmonics with those that are in tune, thereby limiting the number of possibilities (this could, however, be useful to those of you experimenting with microtones and oscillations – use the charts at the back of the book!). What remains are mostly Suspended and/or Minor chords, with a few exceptions. The chords that do use out-of-tune harmonics are in-tune with themselves!

Also worthy of mention is how I went about constructing chords. You must take into consideration that you are the bassist! Pianists and guitarists don't (always) have to include the root into their voicings, but, unless you are planning on performing with a musician that will play that role, the root is a necessity! A typical 3 – 5 – 7 voicing for a C Major chord yields an E minor triad. If you prefer extensions, a 7 – 9 – #11 voicing will give you B minor. I think you get the picture – you have to include the root!

In addition to the tonic, the 3rd and 7th must be included – they determine the chord quality. You are left with a fairly 'pedestrian,' yet stable voicing that clearly represents the harmony. Those who wish to generate their own voicings may use the charts included at the back of the book.

The circled numbers are suggested fingerings, like you would find in guitar literature.

Some partials may be louder than others. Use your ear to balance the chord correctly.

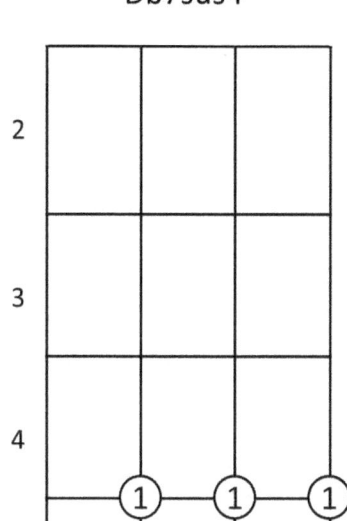

Db7sus4

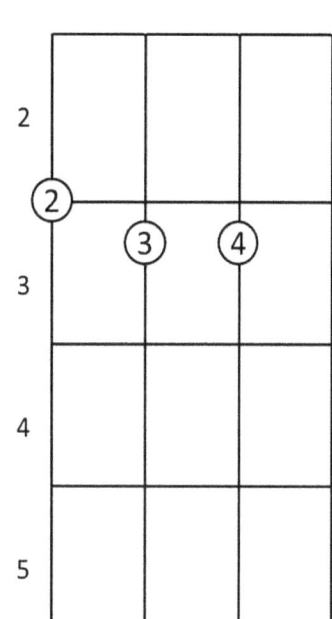

D/F#

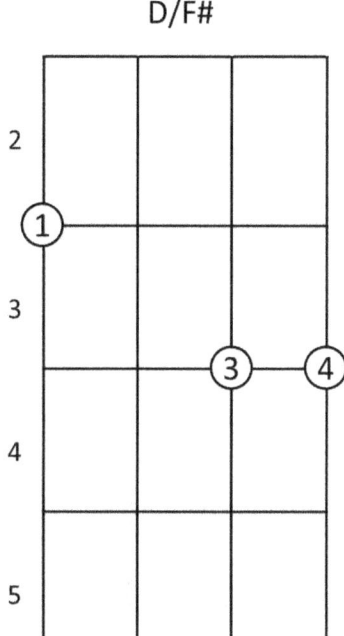

D/F#

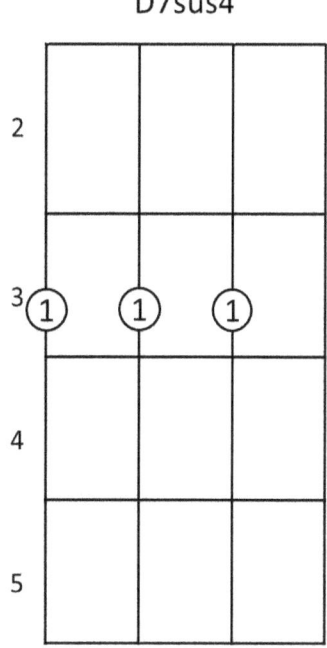

D7sus4

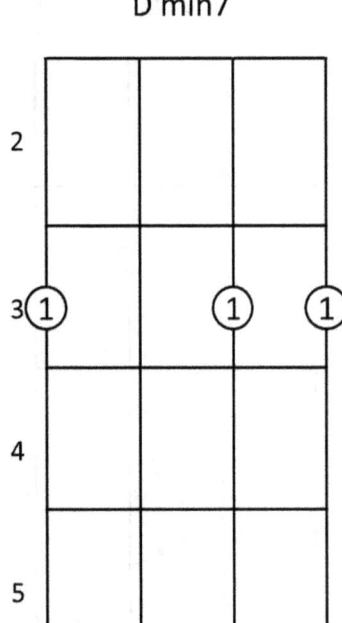
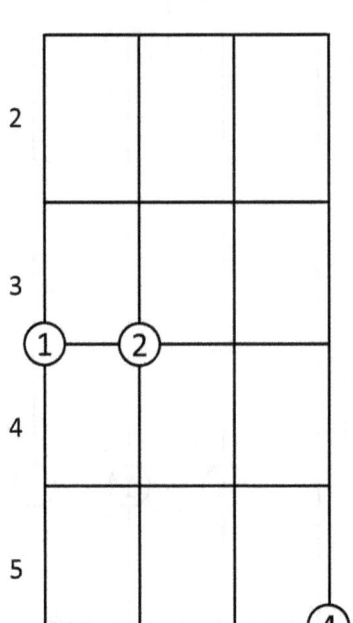
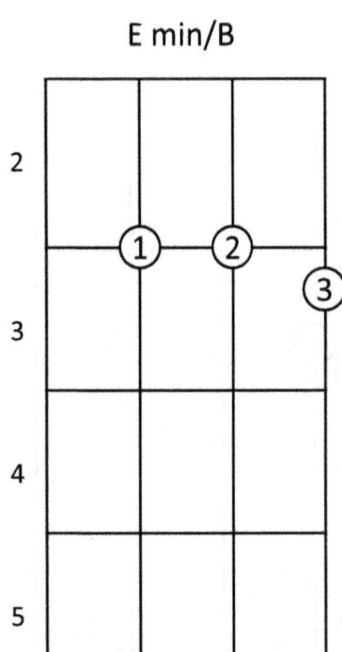
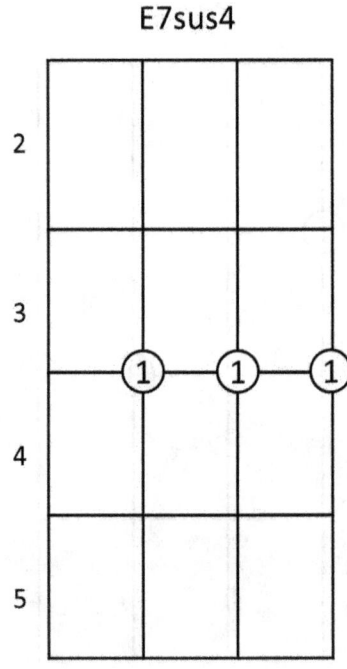

E7sus4
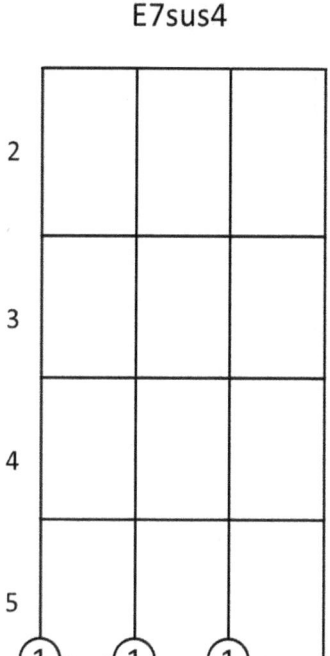

E min7
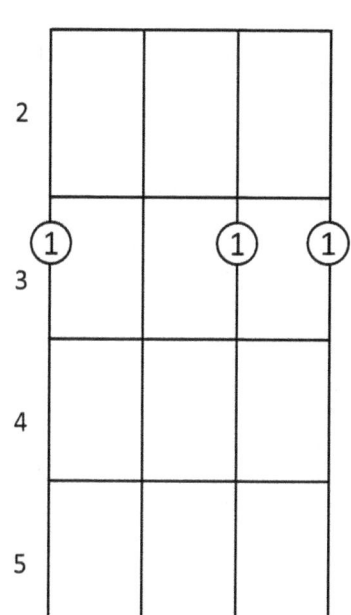

E min7
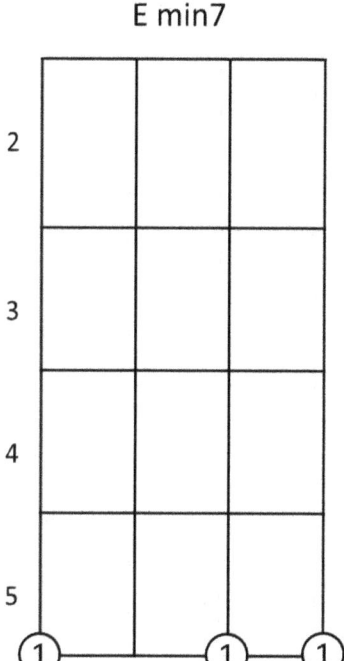

E min7
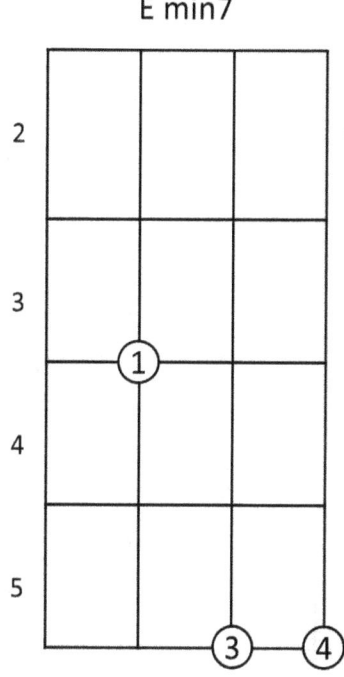

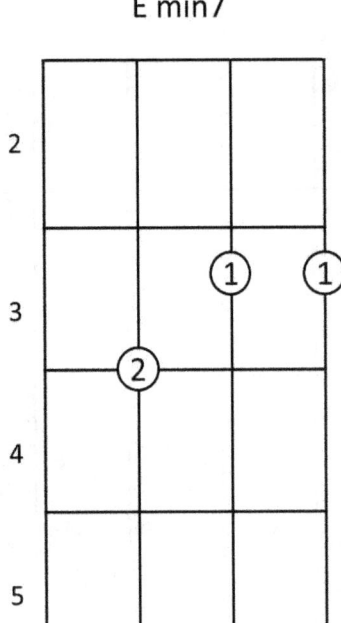
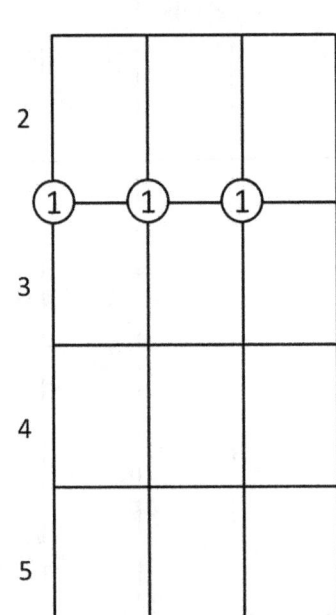
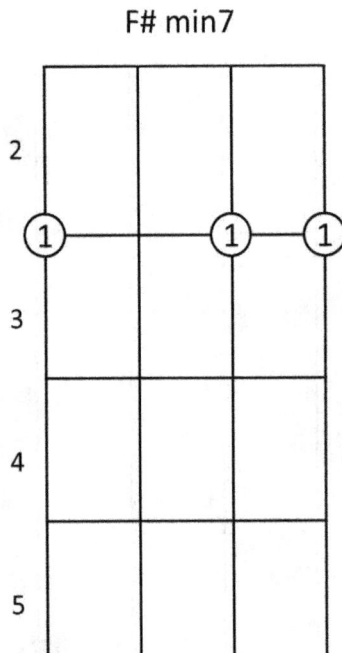
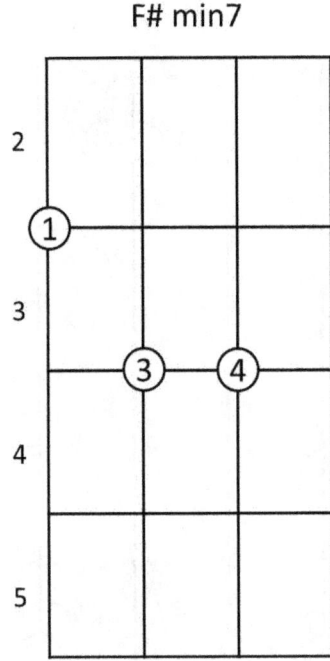

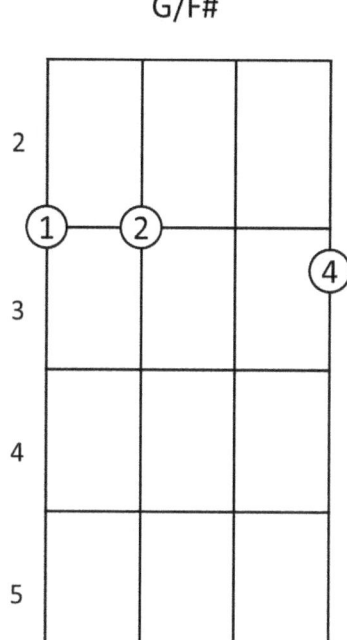

G/F#

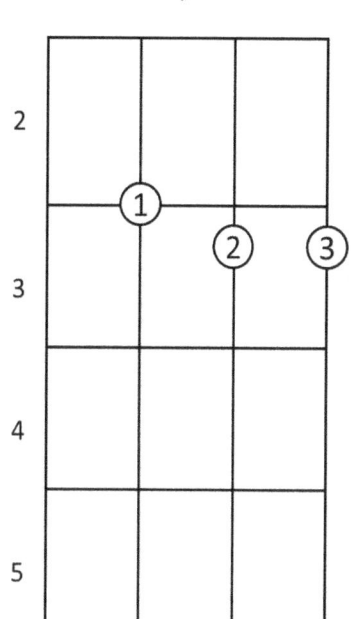

G/B

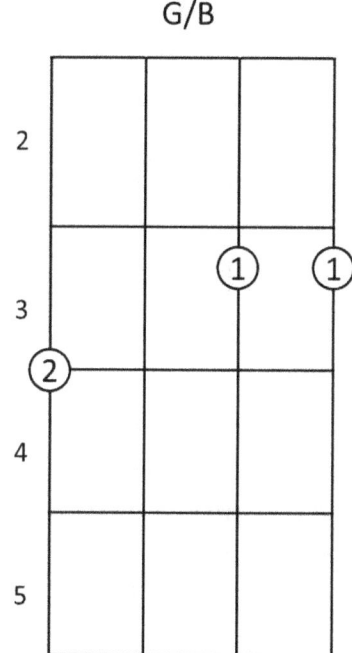

G/B

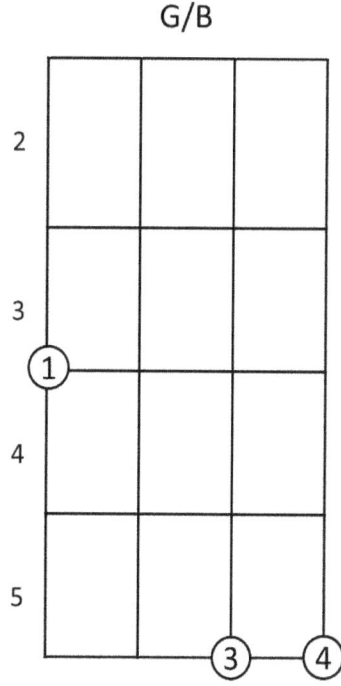

G/B

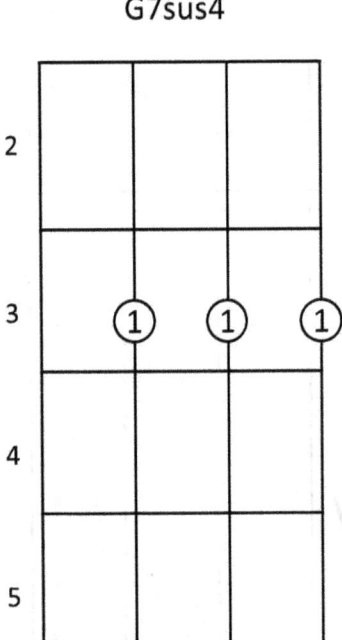

G7sus4

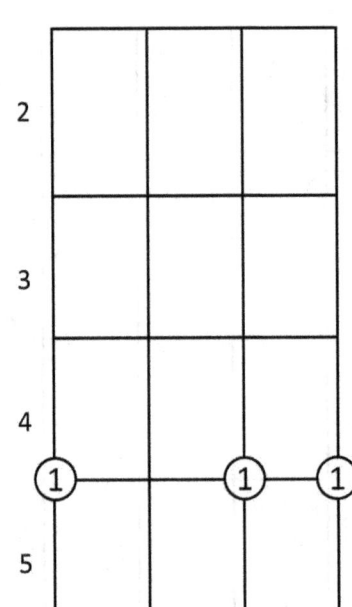

G# min7

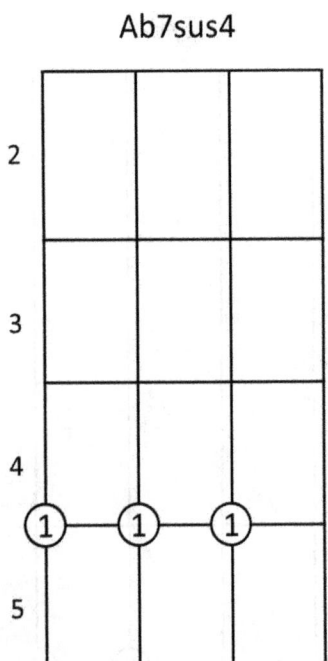

Ab7sus4

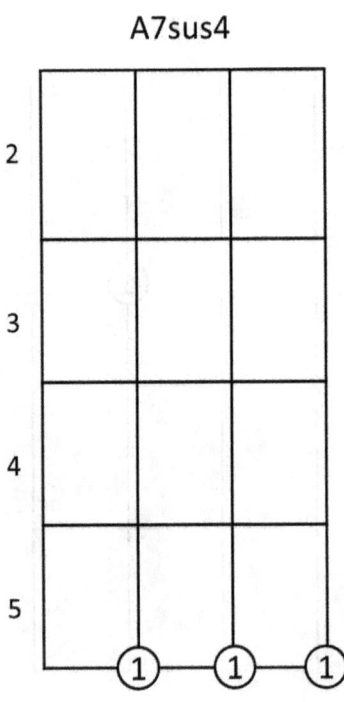

A7sus4

A7sus4

B min/F#
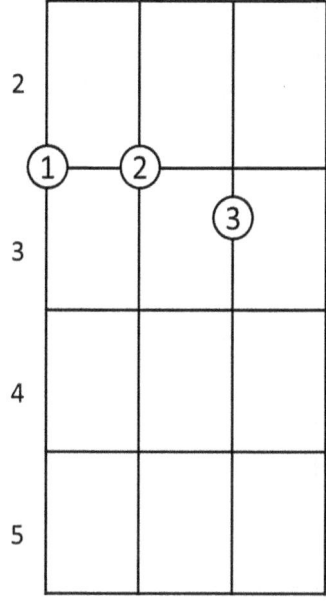

B7sus4
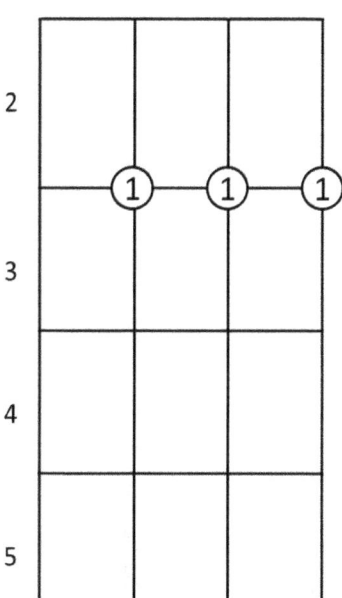

B7sus4
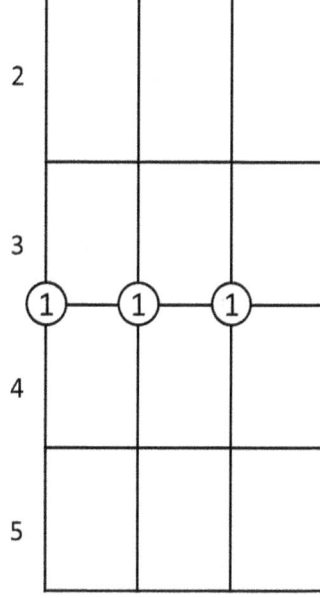

B min7

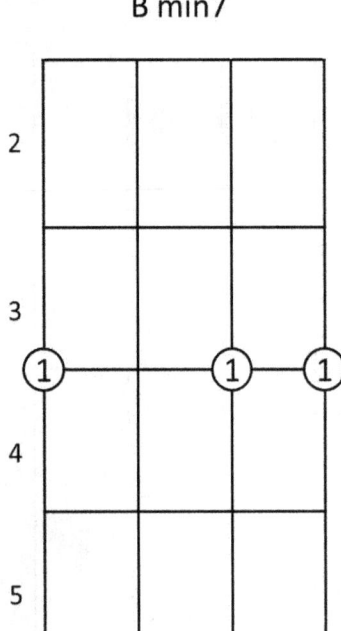

B min7

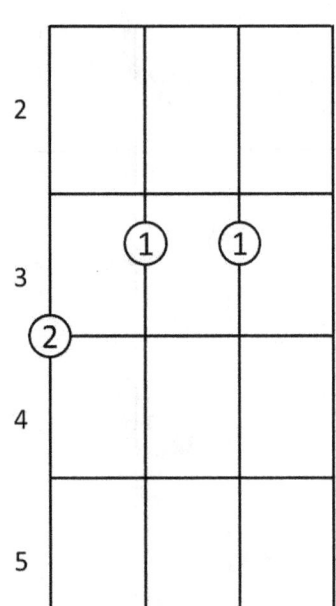

B min7

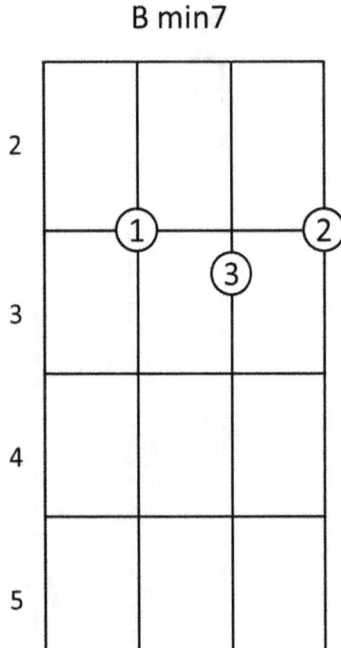

B min7

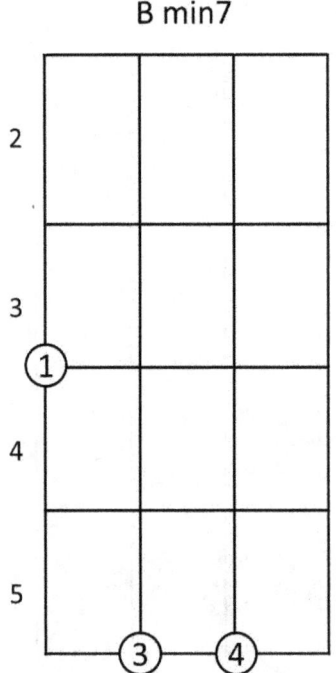

Chords: Chapter 2
2nd Position: Frets 5 - 8

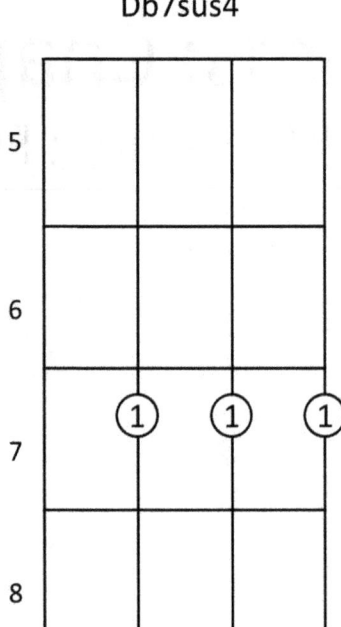
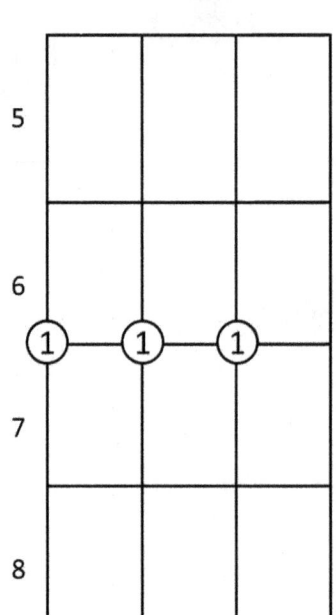
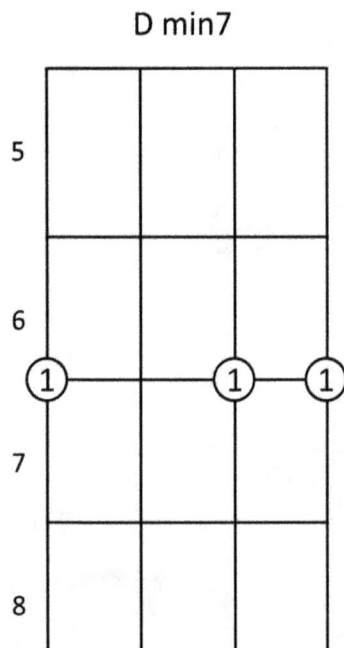
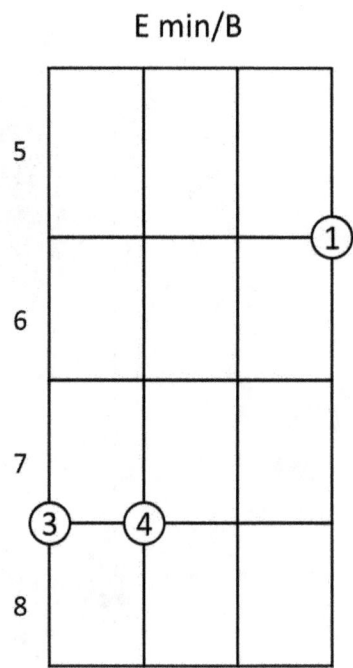

E min/B
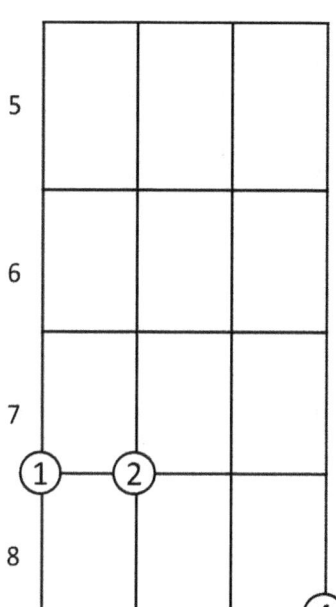

E7sus4
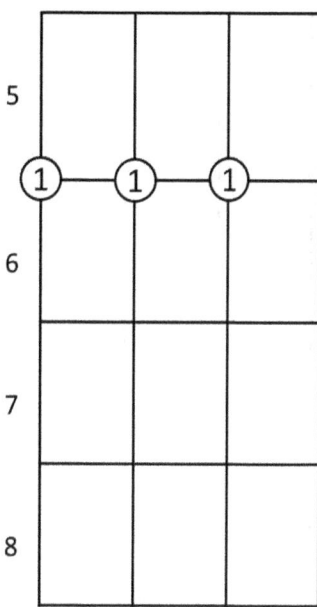

E7sus4
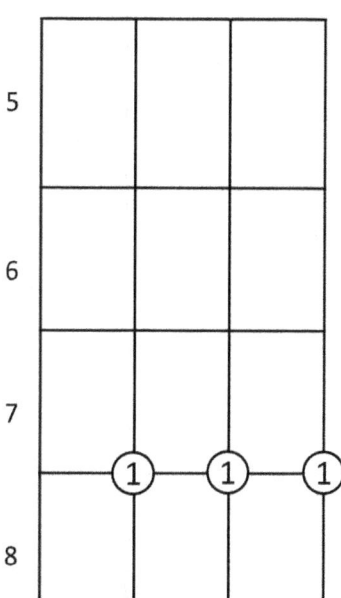

E min7
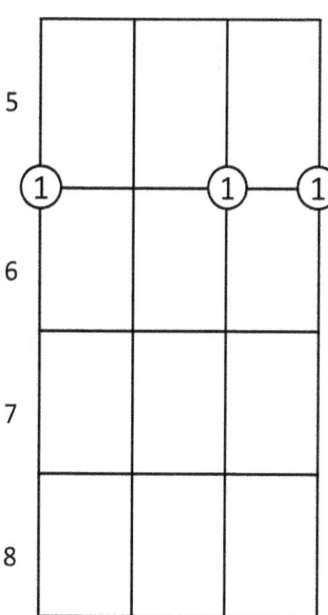

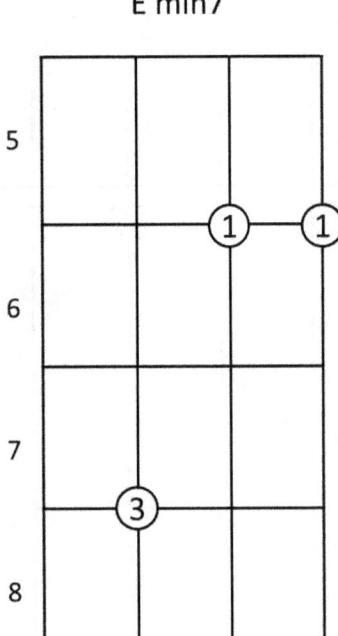
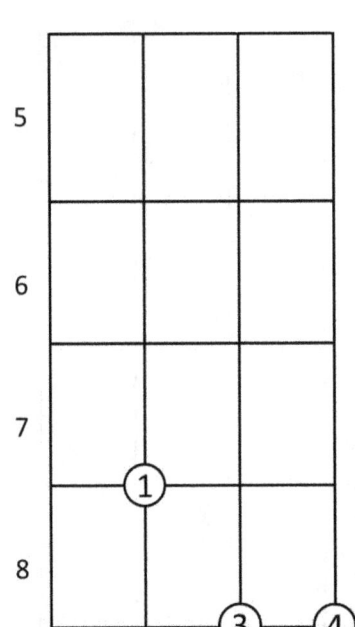
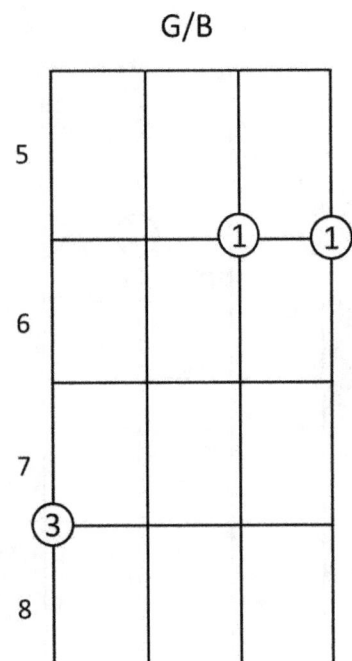
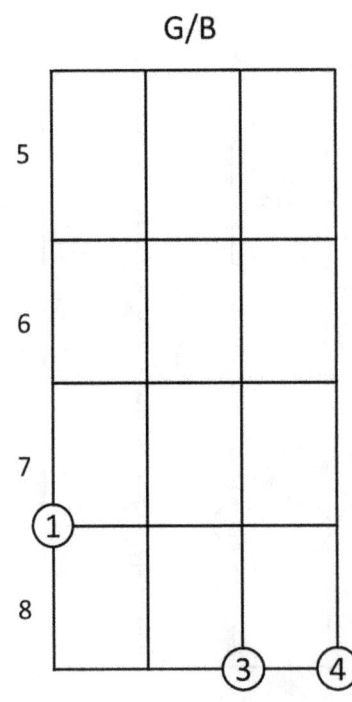

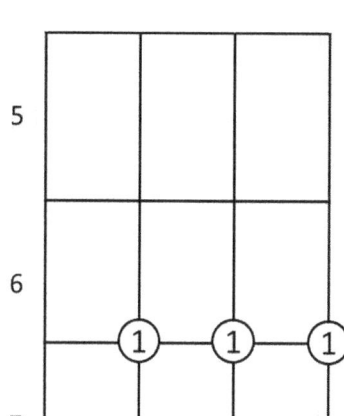

G7sus4

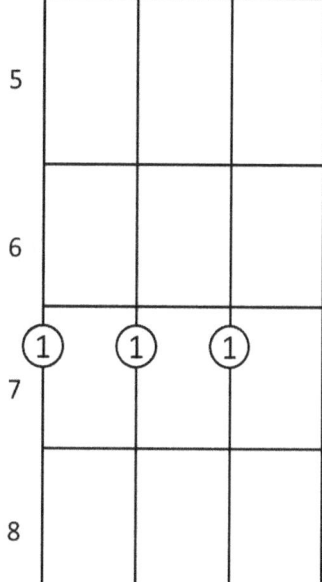

Ab7sus4

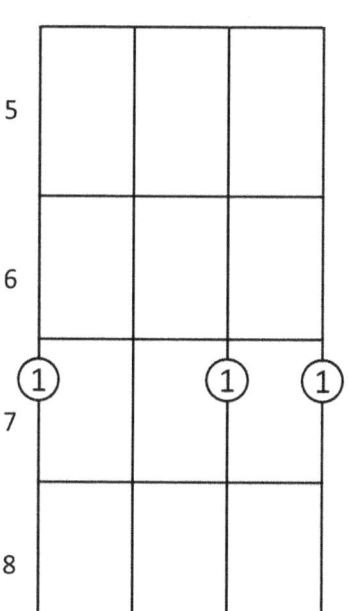

G# min7

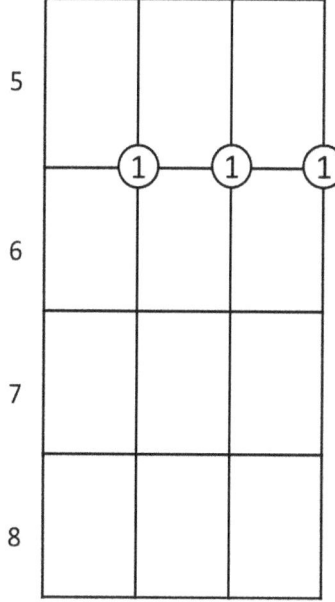

A7sus4

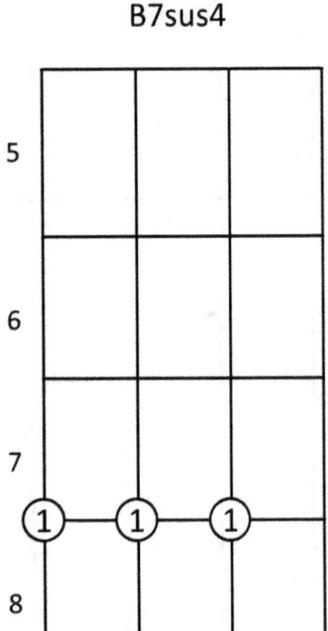
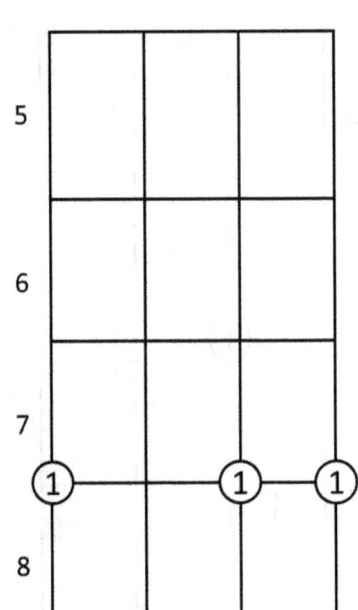
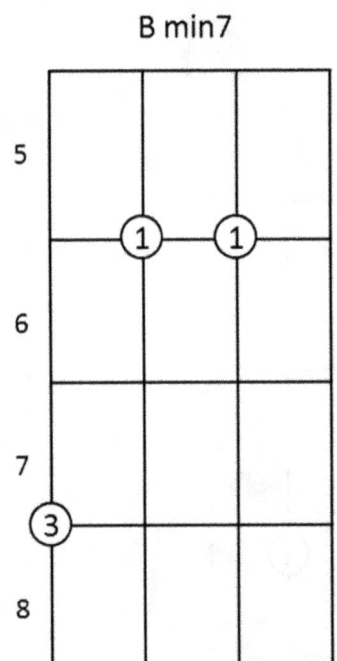

Chords: Chapter 3
3rd Position: Frets 9 - 12

Db7sus4

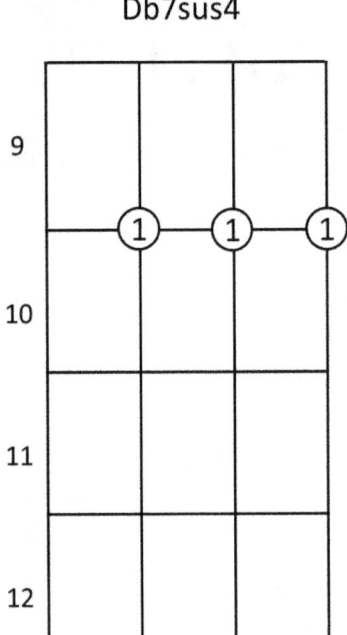

D/F#

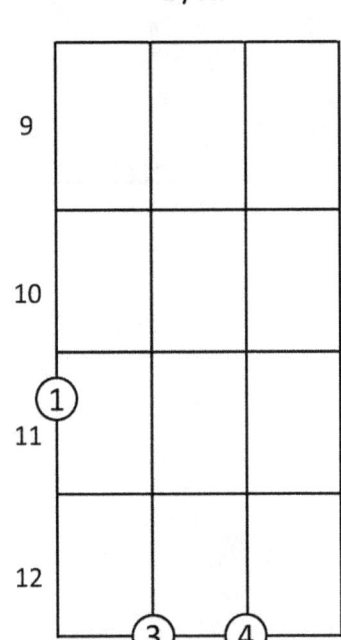

D/F#

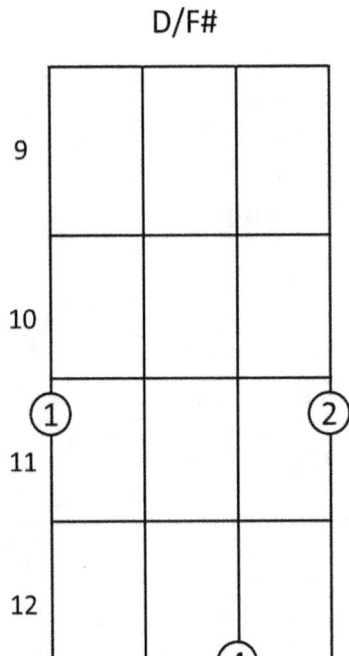

D7sus4

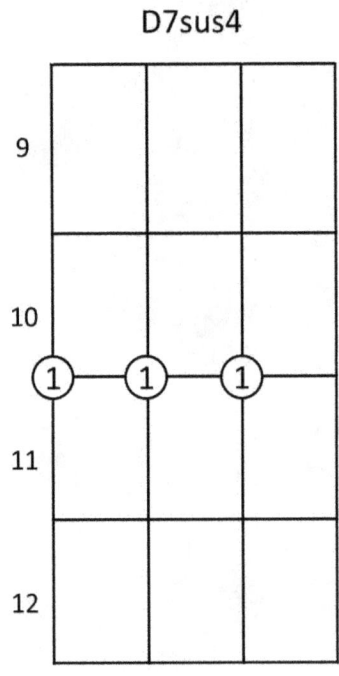

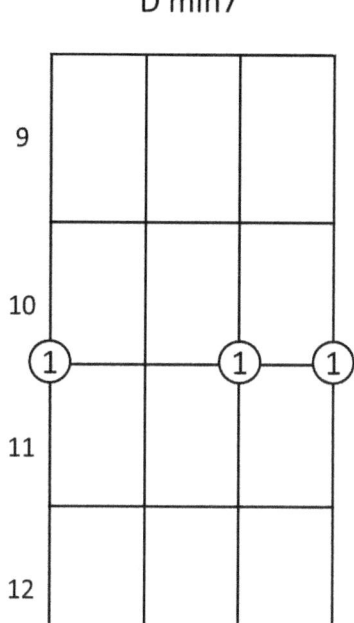

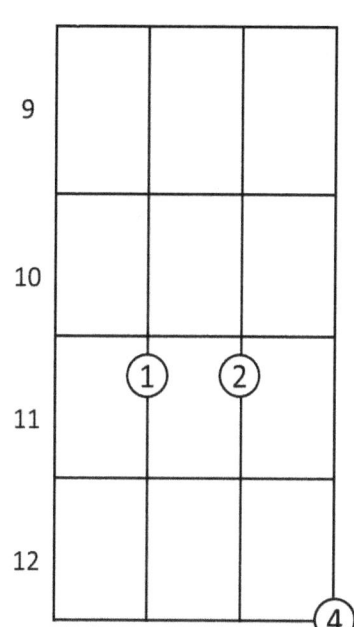

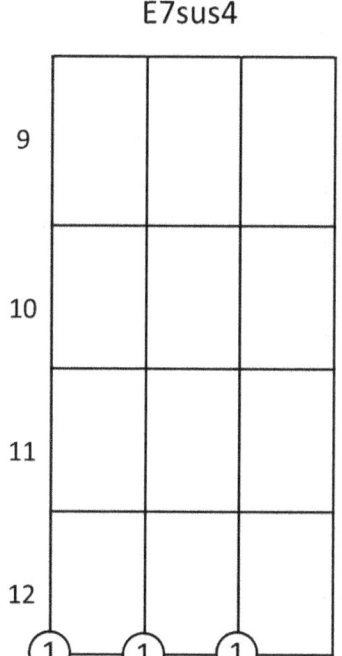

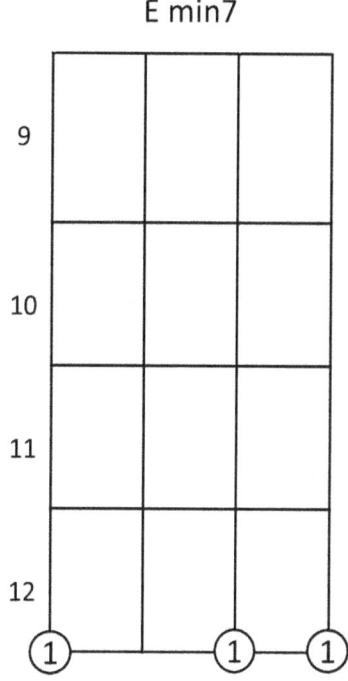

F#7sus4

F# min7
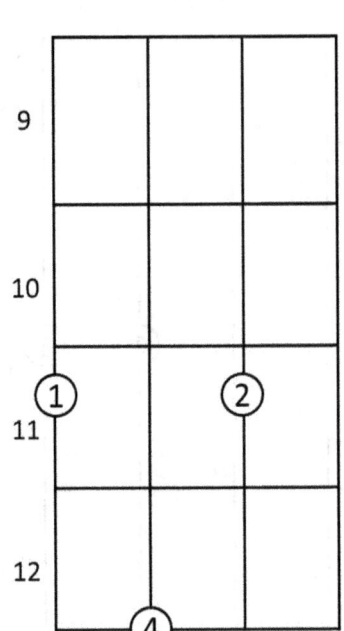

F# min7
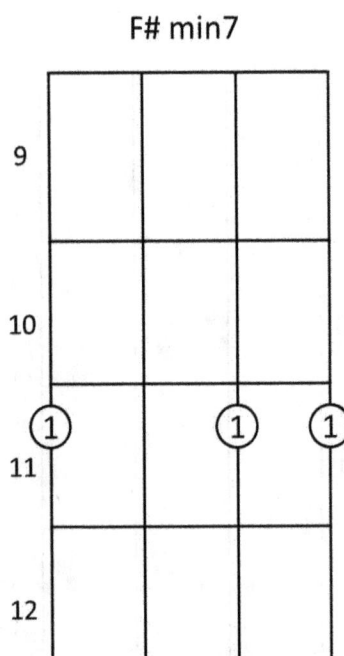

G/B
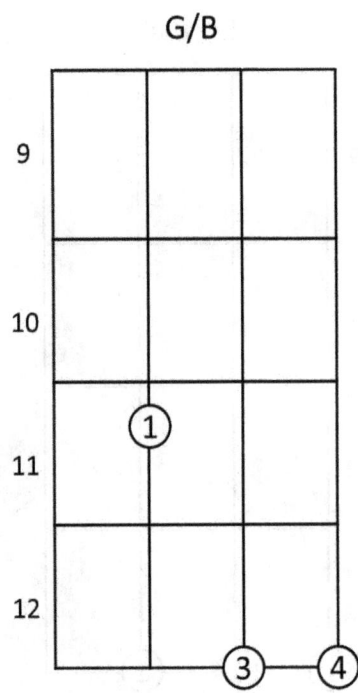

G/F#

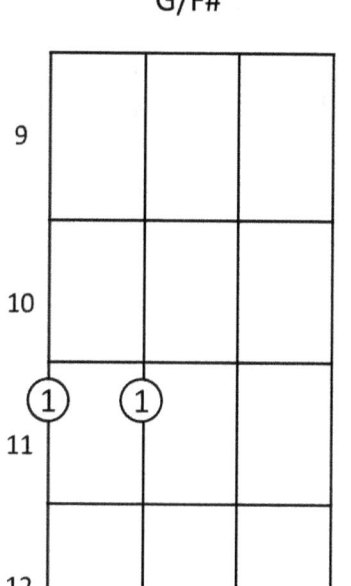

G7sus4

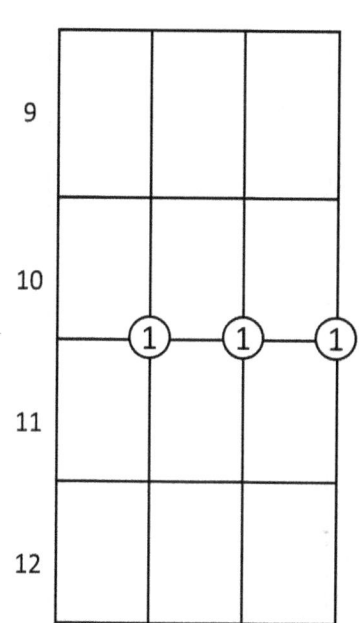

Ab7sus4

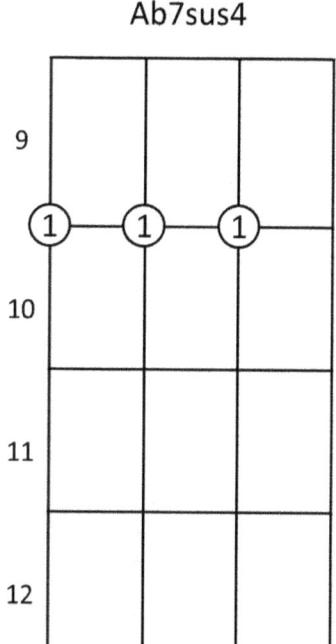

G# min7

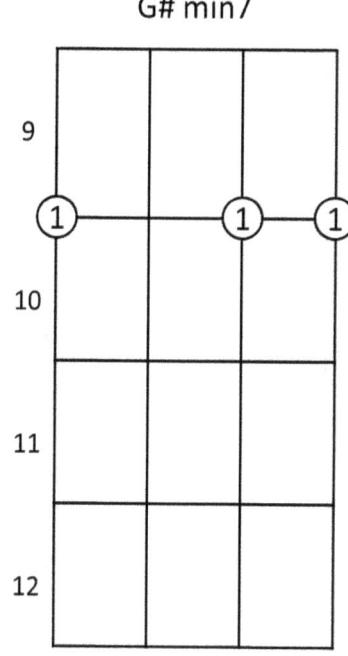

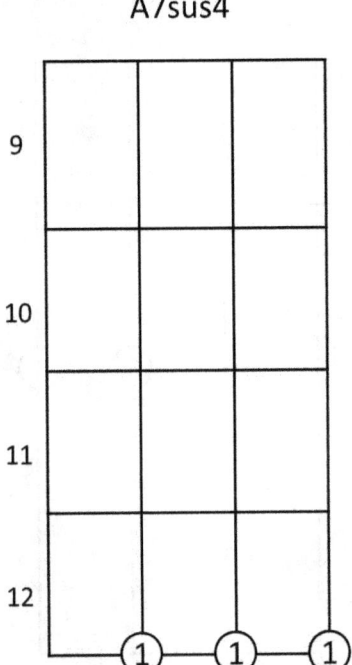
A7sus4

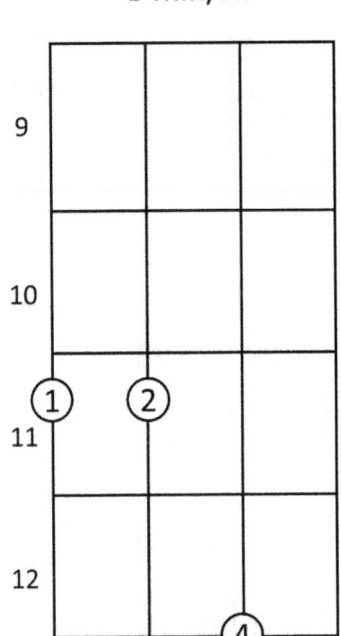
B min/F#

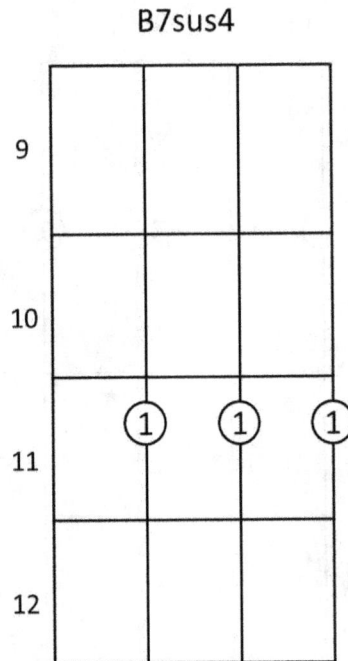
B7sus4

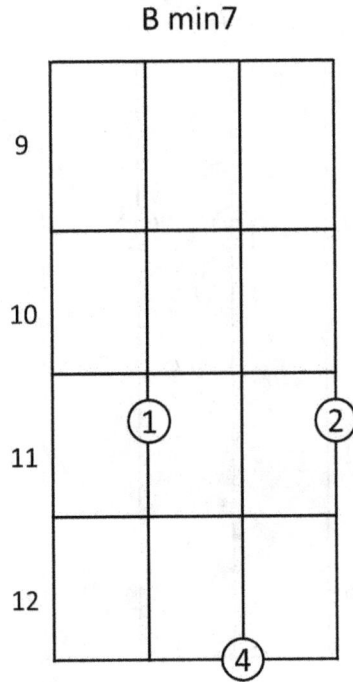
B min7

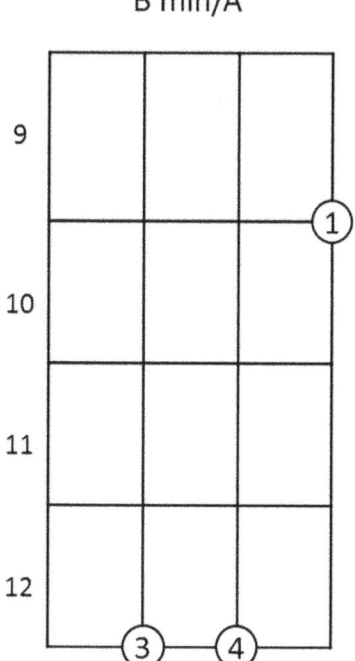

The Etudes
Chapter 1: First Position

C Ionian

Michael Kraft

© 2015 kraftytoonz

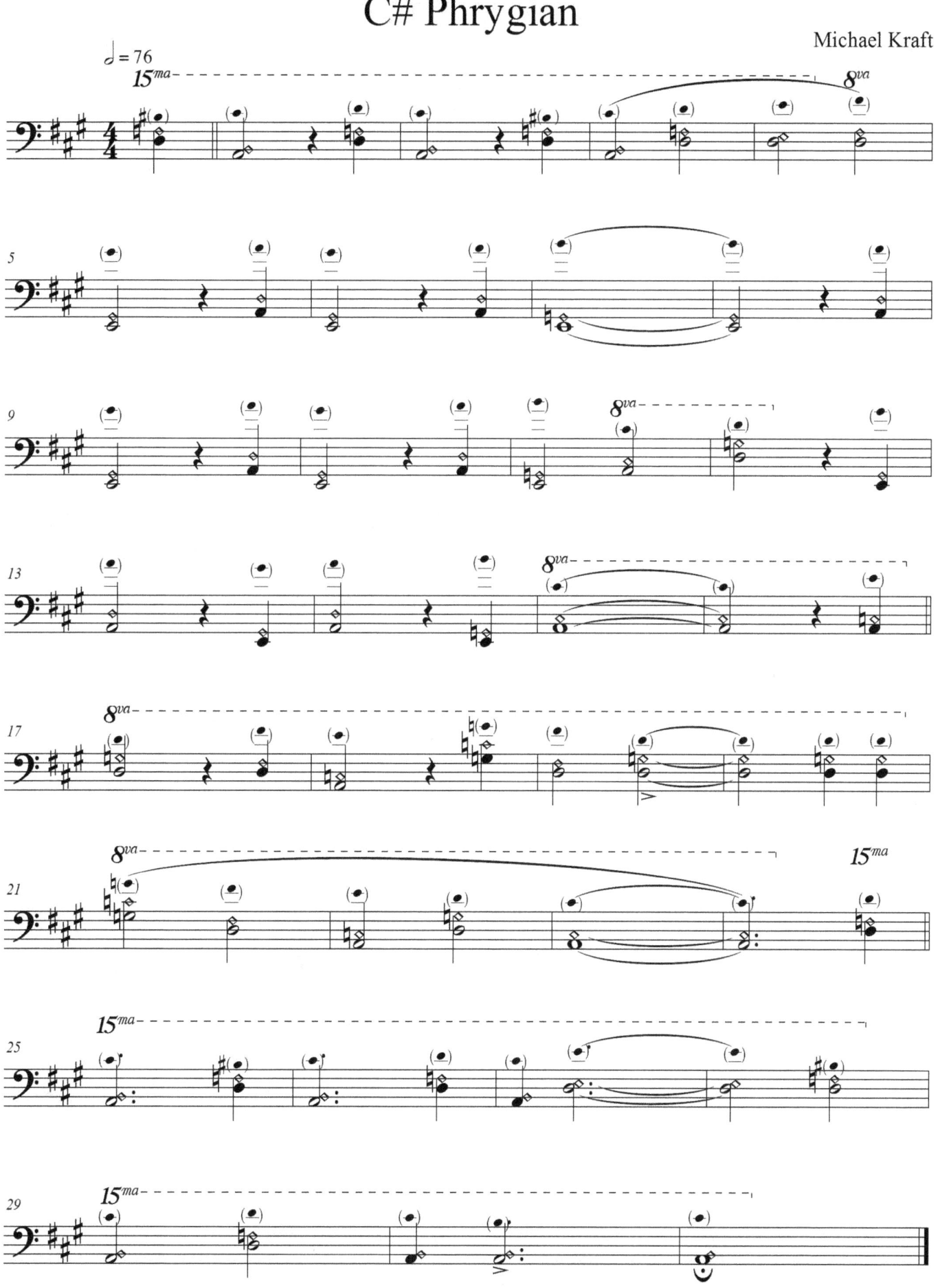

D Mixolydian #11

Michael Kraft

Rubato

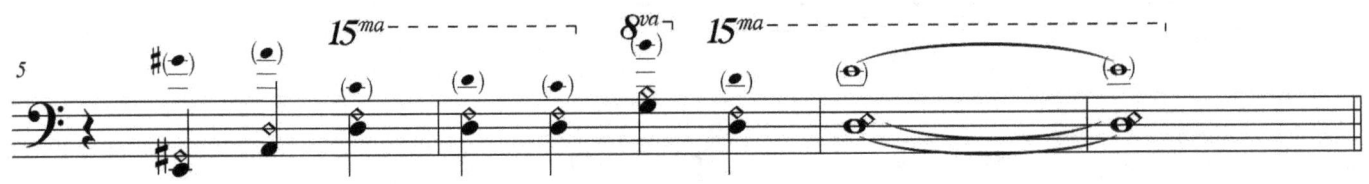

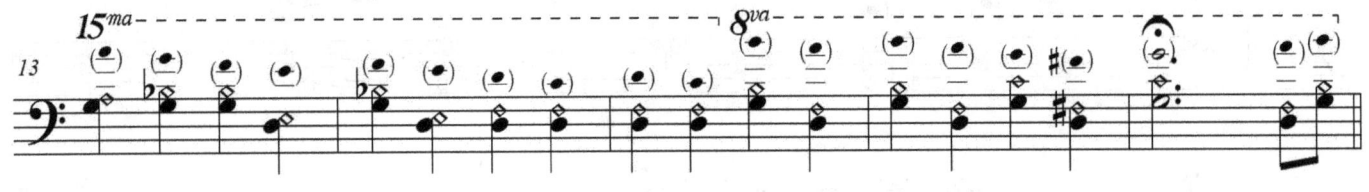

F Lydian

Michael Kraft

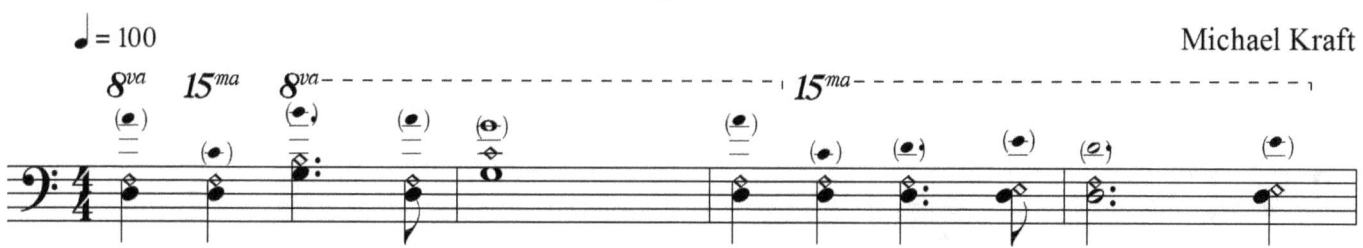
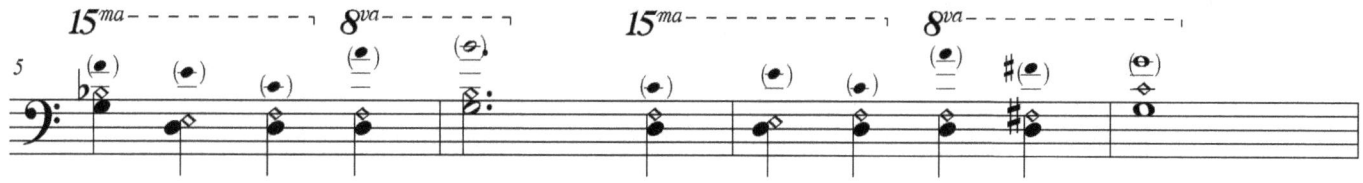
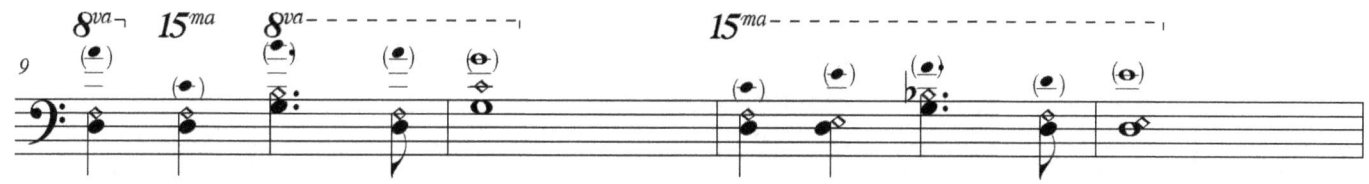
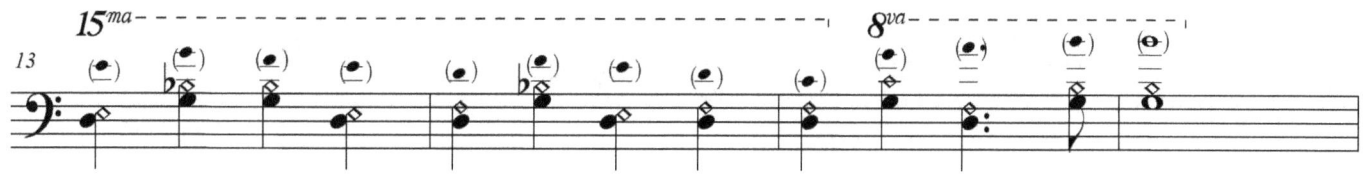

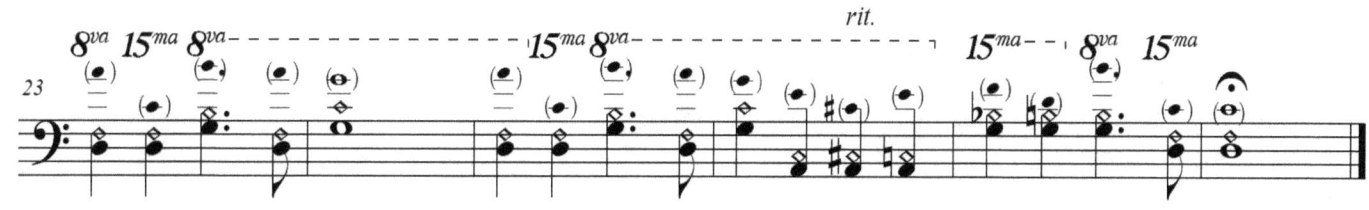

© 2015 kraftytoonz

F# Aeolian

Michael Kraft

The Etudes
Chapter 2: Second Position

Charlie's Waltz

Michael Kraft

© 2015 kraftytoonz

Charlie's Waltz

113

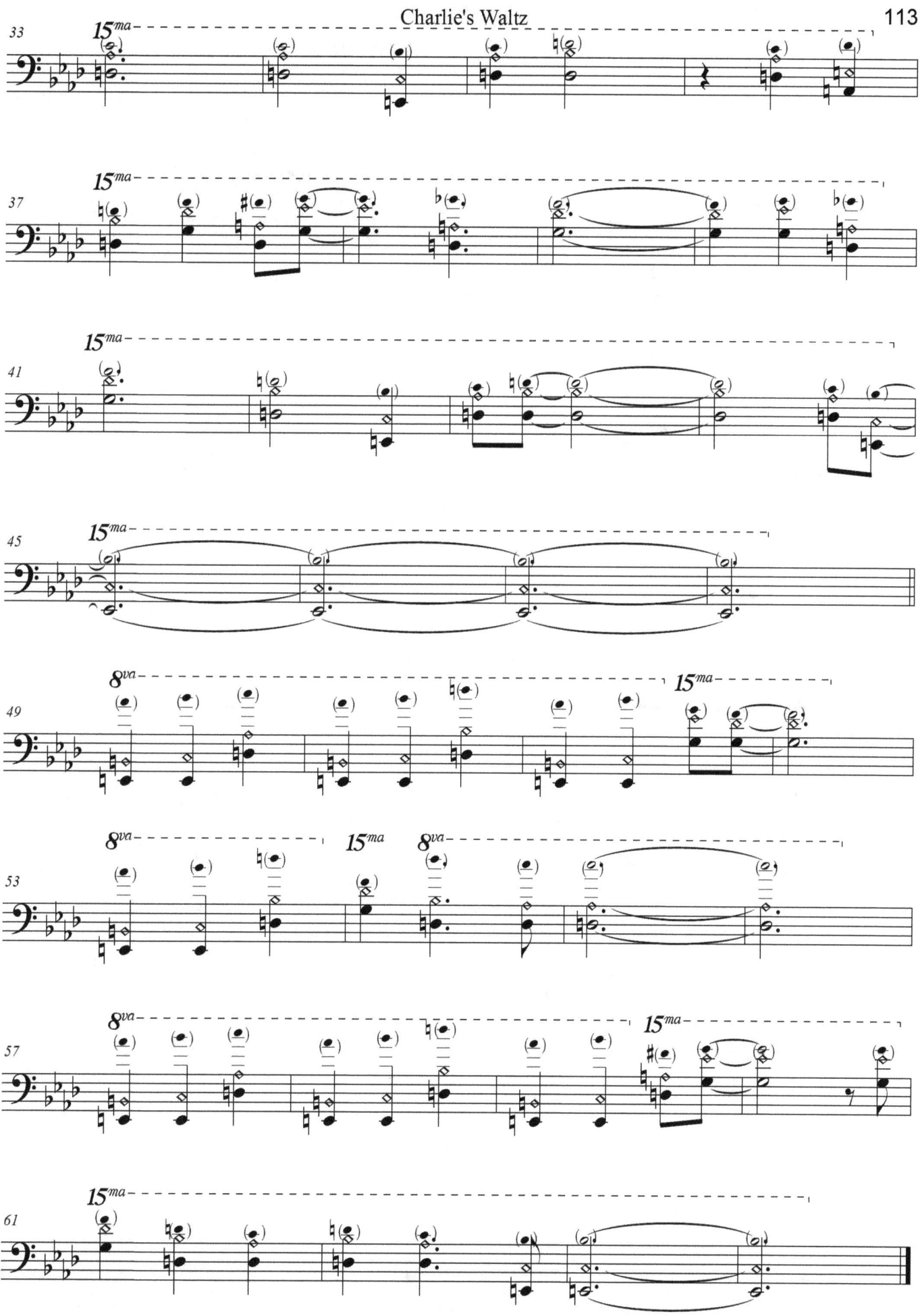

Drunken Carousel

Michael Kraft

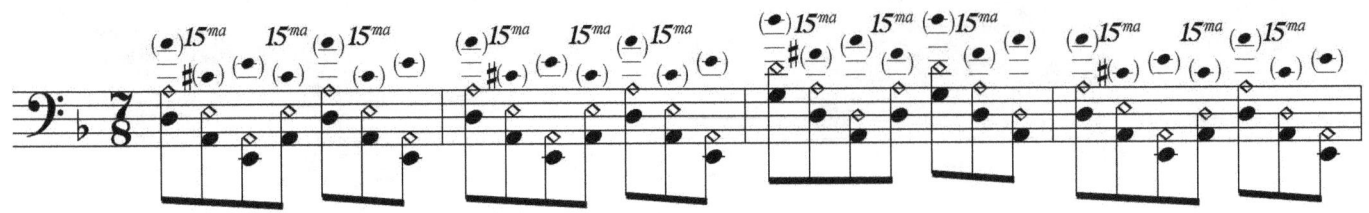
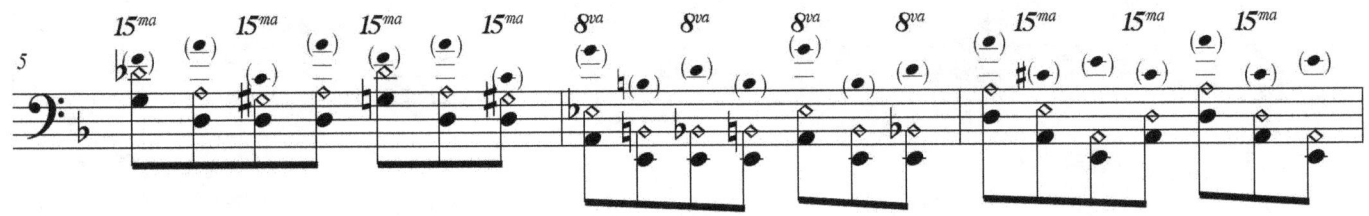
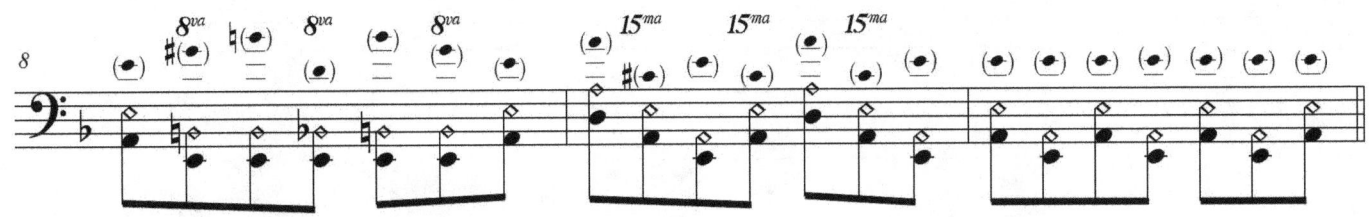
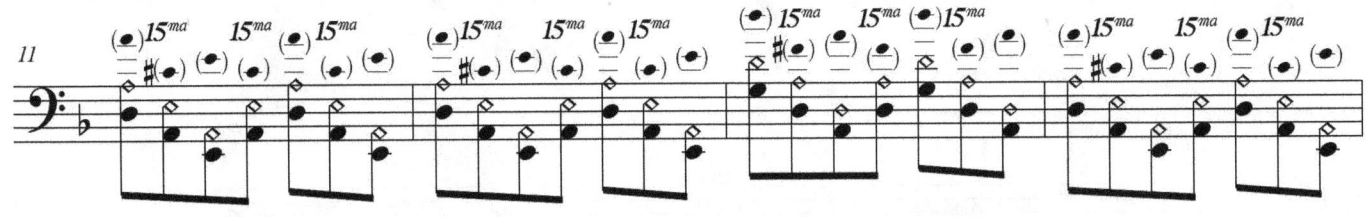
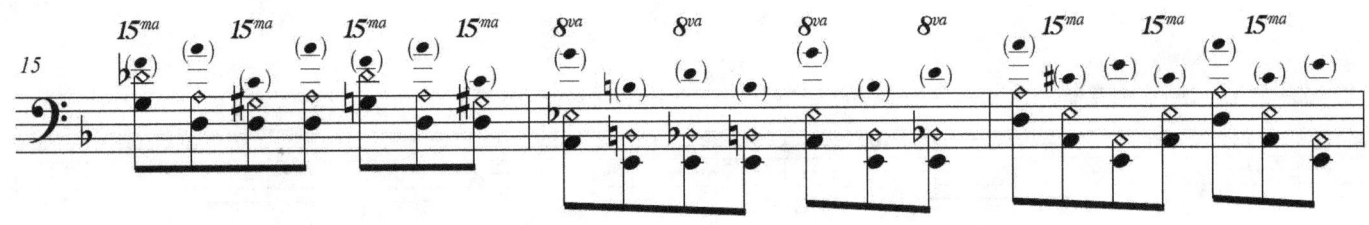
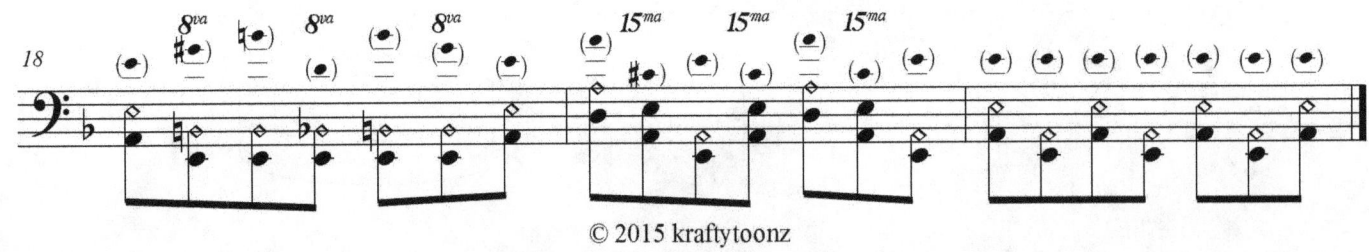

© 2015 kraftytoonz

E Dorian

Michael Kraft

© 2015 kraftytoonz

G Lydian

Michael Kraft

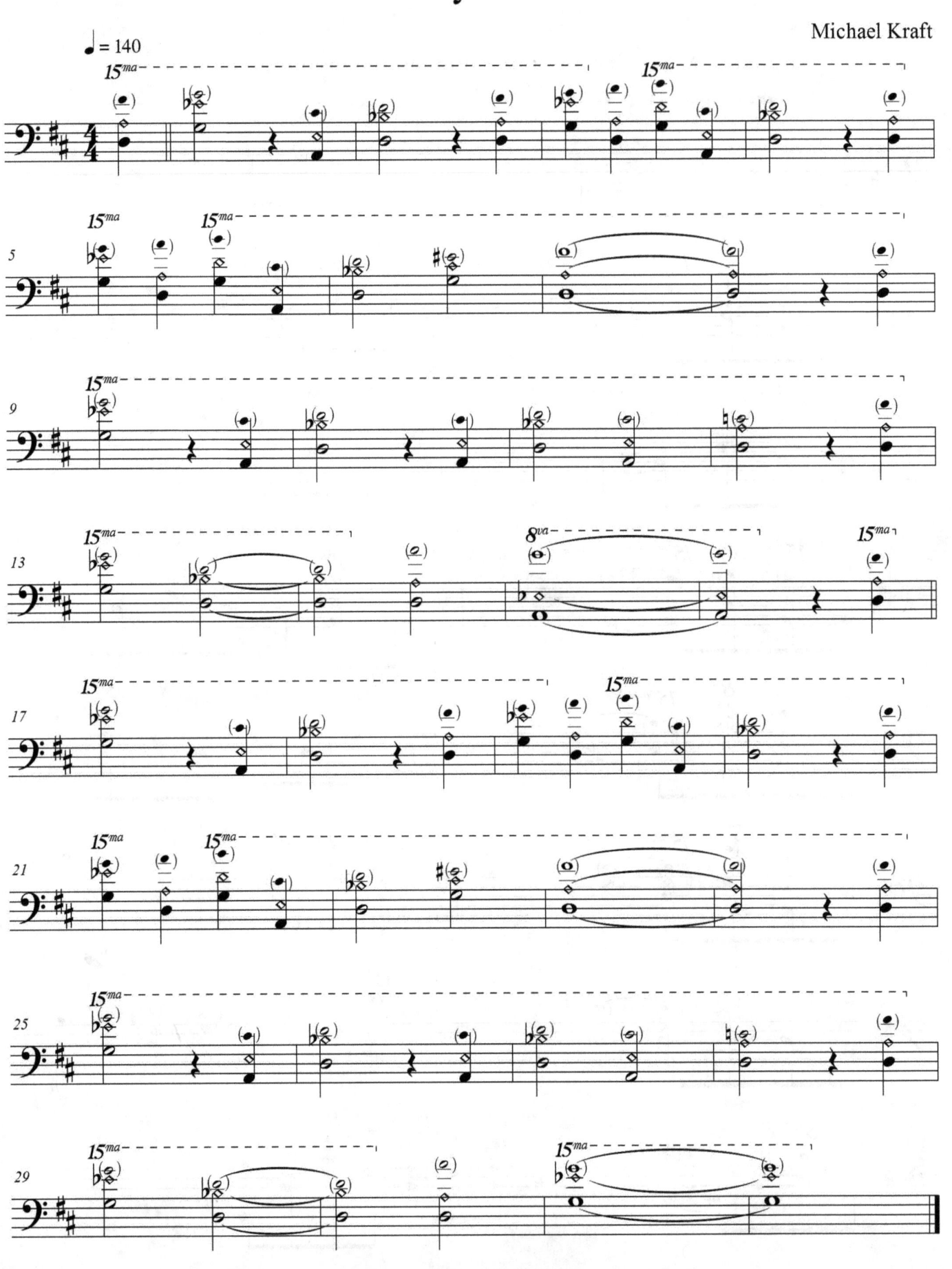

© 2015 kraftytoonz

The Etudes
Chapter 3: Third Position

A Harmonic Minor

Michael Kraft

© 2015 kraftytoonz

A Mixolydian

Michael Kraft

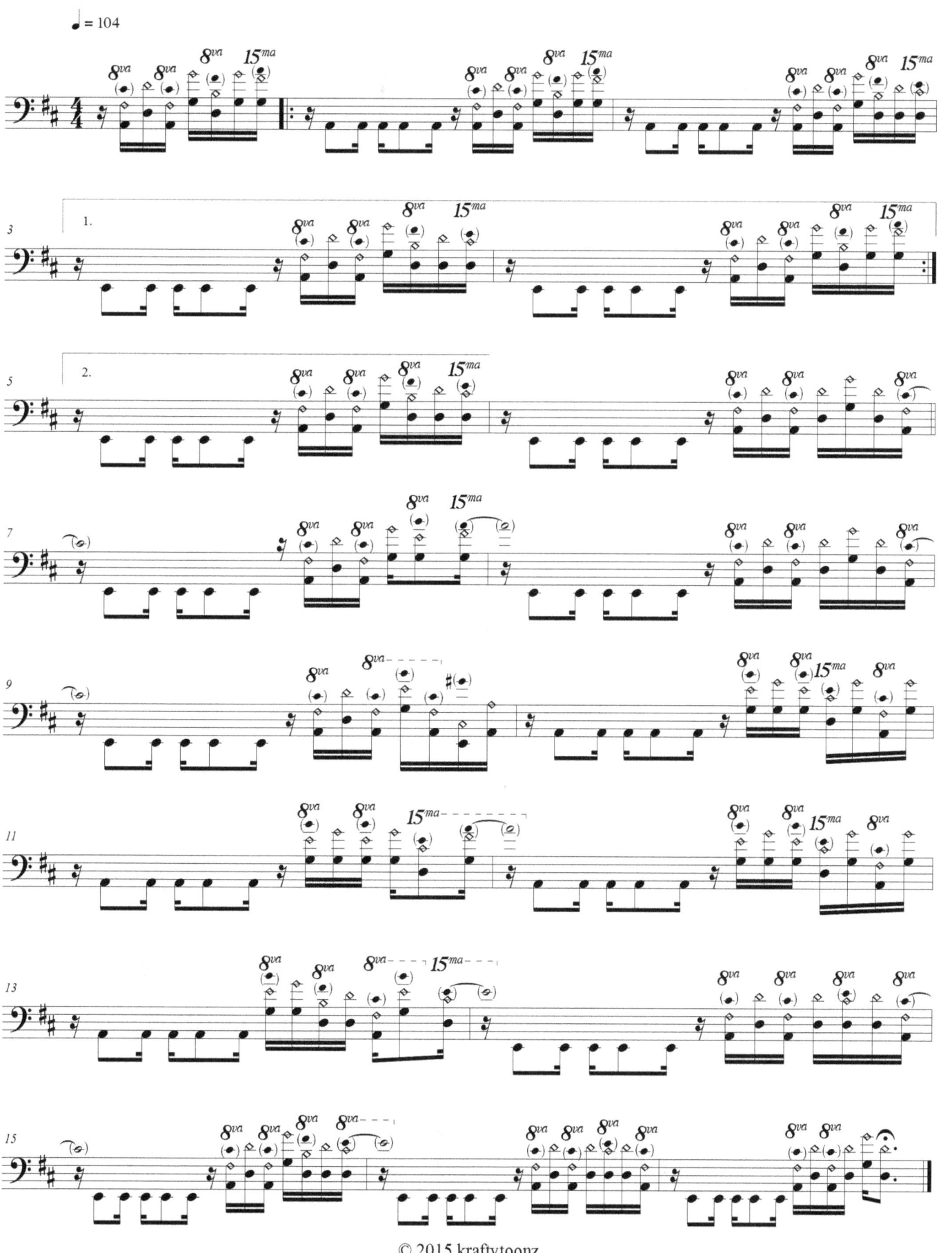

© 2015 kraftytoonz

B Locrian

Michael Kraft

© 2015 kraftytoonz

Eerie Film Scene

Michael Kraft

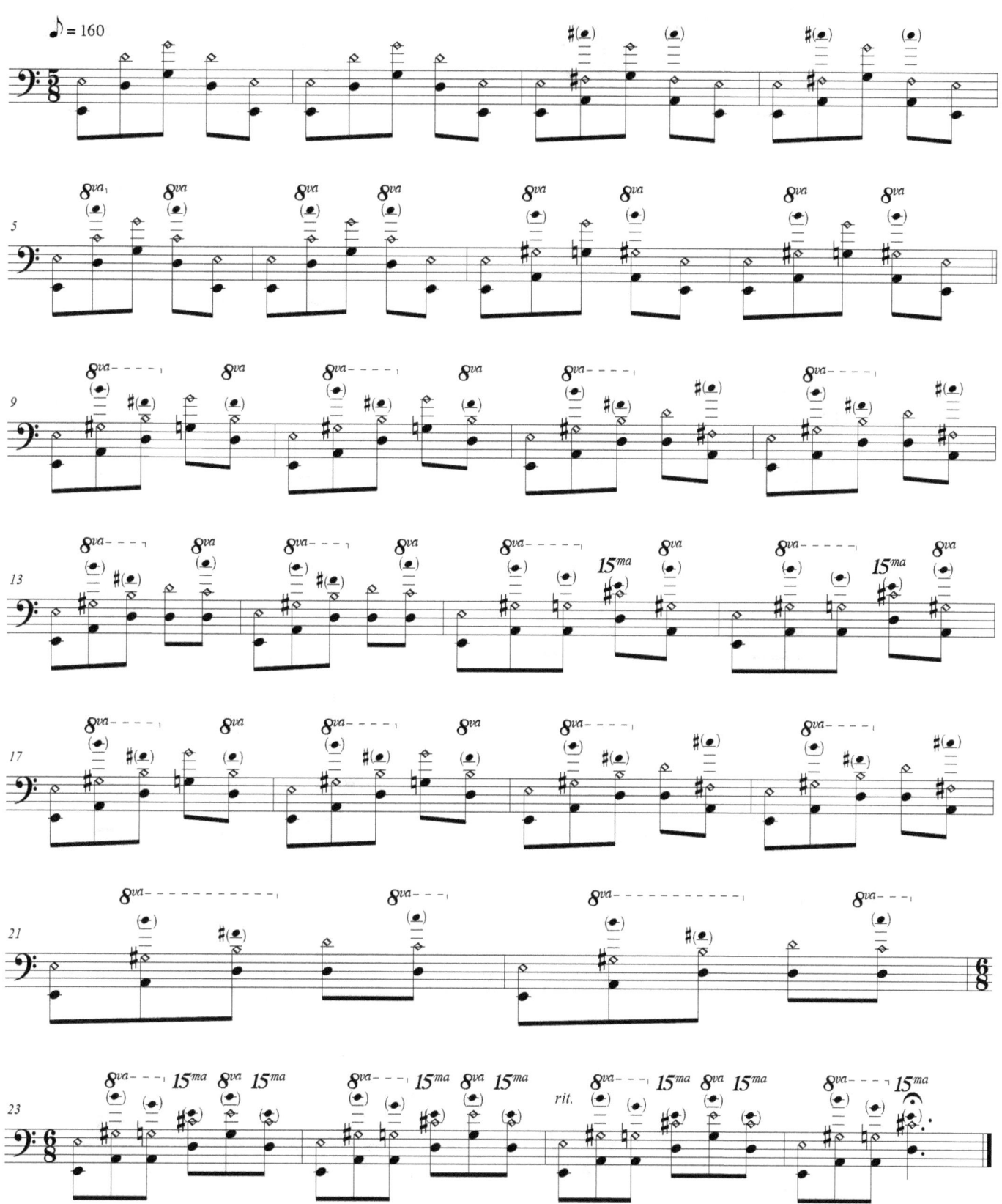

© 2015 kraftytoonz

C Ionian

Michael Kraft

Conclusion

By now you should feel comfortable with harmonics. As I mentioned in the Introduction, it doesn't matter how you learn them (by their appearance in the harmonic series versus their relationship to the fretted notes on the fingerboard), but that you fully grasp the concept and are able to locate them with ease. That being said, do try to memorize the 3rd and 5th frets. They contain the most harmonics, and because they are located on a part the fingerboard that you should be familiar with, can be incorporated into your playing with little effort.

For the purpose of giving you a visual and aural point of reference to accompany the written page, I will be uploading videos of myself performing the Etudes. They will published on my YouTube Channel (Michael Kraft – kraftytoonz) in the coming months. Please subscribe to the channel and check for updates soon!

Your mission, should you choose to accept it, is to free yourself from the Positions, incorporate the entire fingerboard into your playing and to make music! With the proper musical training, the right amount of personal ambition and the book that you hold in your hands, you should be capable of creating the next *Portrait of Tracy* or arranging another *Amazing Grace*. Go for it!

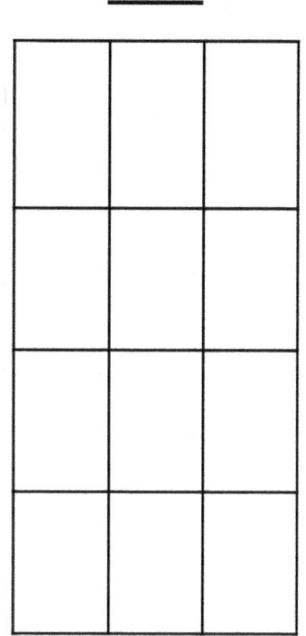
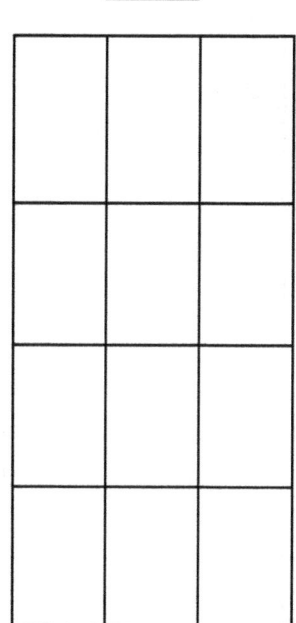
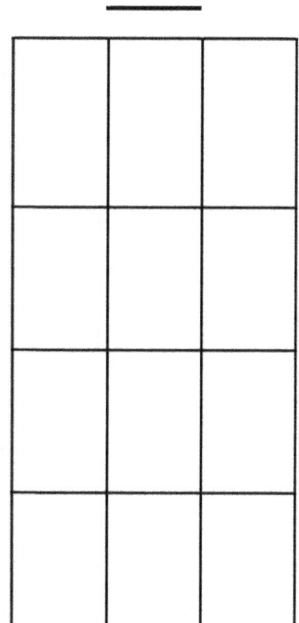
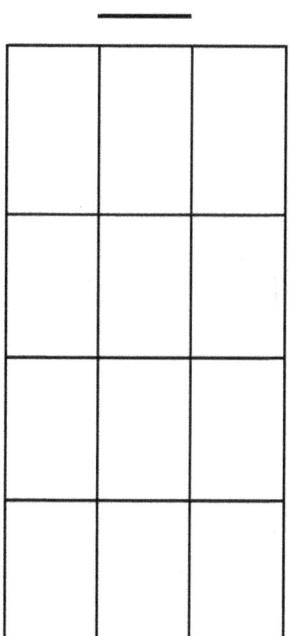

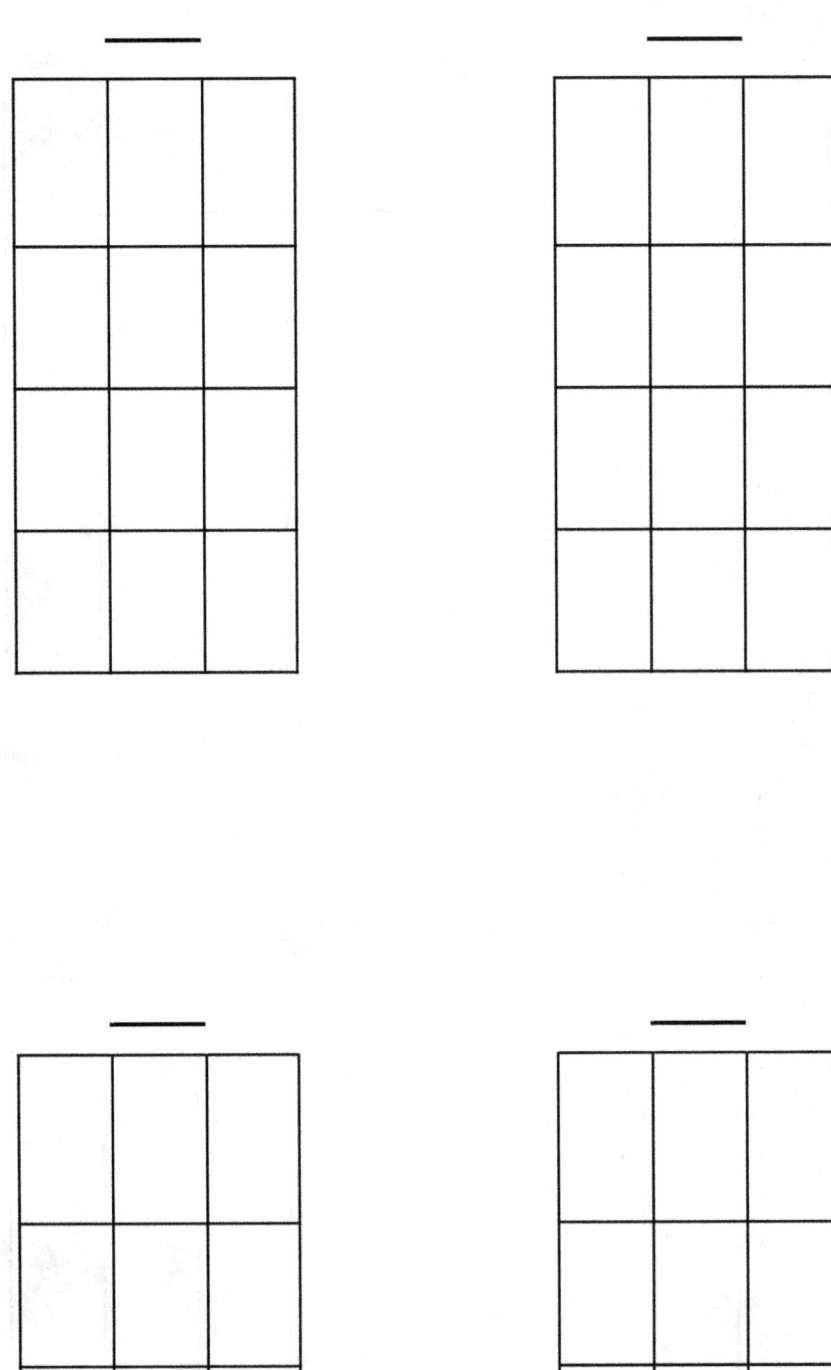

www.ingramcontent.com/pod-product-compliance
Lightning Source LLC
Chambersburg PA
CBHW080346170426
43194CB00014B/2700